Selected Books of the Beloved

Also by Gregory Orr

POETRY

The Last Love Poem I Will Ever Write (W.W. Norton, 2019)

River Inside the River (W.W. Norton, 2013)

How Beautiful the Beloved (Copper Canyon Press, 2008)

Concerning the Book That Is the Body of the Beloved
(Copper Canyon Press, 2005)

The Caged Owl: New and Selected Poems
(Copper Canyon Press, 2002)

Orpheus & Eurydice (Copper Canyon Press, 2001)

City of Salt (University of Pittsburgh Press, 1995)

New and Selected Poems (Wesleyan University Press, 1988)

We Must Make a Kingdom of It
(Wesleyan University Press, 1986)

The Red House (Harper & Row, 1980)

Gathering the Bones Together (Harper & Row, 1975)

Burning the Empty Nests (Harper & Row, 1973)

CRITICISM

A Primer for Poets & Readers of Poetry (W.W. Norton, 2018)

Poetry as Survival (University of Georgia Press, 2002)

Poets Teaching Poets: Self and the World
(edited by Voigt and Orr, University of Michigan Press, 1996)

Richer Entanglements: Essays and Notes on Poetry and Poems
(University of Michigan Press, 1993)

Stanley Kunitz: An Introduction to the Poetry
(Columbia University Press, 1985)

MEMOIR

The Blessing (Milkweed Editions, 2018)

Selected Books of the Beloved

Gregory Orr

COPPER CANYON PRESS

PORT TOWNSEND, WASHINGTON

Cover art: Takahiko Hayashi, *The Nest of Winds, 6cu* (detail), 2014, etching, chine collé, edition of 10, 17.75 × 12 inches. Courtesy of the artist and Froelick Gallery, Portland, Oregon.

Copper Canyon Press is in residence at Fort Worden State Park in Port Townsend, Washington, under the auspices of Centrum. Centrum is a gathering place for artists and creative thinkers from around the world, students of all ages and backgrounds, and audiences seeking extraordinary cultural enrichment.

LIBRARY OF CONGRESS CATALOGING-IN-PUBLICATION DATA
Names: Orr, Gregory, author.
Title: Selected books of the beloved / poems by Gregory Orr.
Description: Port Townsend, Washington : Copper Canyon Press, 2022. | Includes index. | Summary: "A collection of poems by Gregory Orr"— Provided by publisher.
Identifiers: LCCN 2021055238 | ISBN 9781556596537 (paperback) | ISBN 9781619322561 (epub)
Subjects: LCGFT: Poetry.
Classification: LCC PS3565.R7 S45 2022 | DDC 811/.54—dc23
LC record available at https://lccn.loc.gov/2021055238

98765432 FIRST PRINTING

COPPER CANYON PRESS
Post Office Box 271
Port Townsend, Washington 98368
www.coppercanyonpress.org

Acknowledgments

Some of the poems in this collection appeared previously in literary journals *The American Poetry Review, Plume,* and *Smartish Pace* and in Copper Canyon Press volumes *The Caged Owl, Concerning the Book That Is the Body of the Beloved,* and *How Beautiful the Beloved.* Poems also appeared in *River Inside the River: Poems,* by Gregory Orr (copyright 2013 by Gregory Orr), and *The Last Love Poem I Will Ever Write: Poems,* by Gregory Orr (copyright 2019 by Gregory Orr), used by permission of W.W. Norton & Company Inc.

for Trisha, always

Contents

PART ONE

FROM The Book of Loss and Grief

FROM The First Book of the Book

Part One: The Book of the Resurrection of the Beloved Imaged as the Story of Isis and Osiris

Part Two: The Book of the Body of the Beloved
Imaged as a City Made of Poems

FROM The First Book of Singing, Which Is
the Book of Resurrection of the Beloved

PART TWO

FROM The First Book of the World, Which Is the Book of Changes

FROM The Book of Searching, Which Is
the Book of Risk

PART THREE

FROM The Book of the Body of the Beloved, Which Is Also the Second Book of Singing

FROM The Book of Reading and Writing,
Which Is the Book of Poets and Poems

PART FOUR

FROM The Book of Words, Which Is the Book of Listening and Speaking

CopperCanyonPress.org

BUSINESS REPLY MAIL

FIRST-CLASS MAIL   PERMIT NO. 43   PORT TOWNSEND WA

POSTAGE WILL BE PAID BY ADDRESSEE

Copper Canyon Press
PO Box 271
Port Townsend, WA 98368-9931

What do you think?

MAIL THIS CARD, SHARE YOUR COMMENTS ON FACEBOOK OR TWITTER,
OR EMAIL POETRY@COPPERCANYONPRESS.ORG

OUR MISSION:

Poetry is vital to language and
living, Copper Canyon Press
publishes extraordinary poetry
from around the world to
engage the imaginations and
intellects of readers.

Thank you for your thoughts!

BOOK TITLE: _____

COMMENTS: _____

Can we quote you? ☐ yes ☐ no

☐ Please send me a catalog full of poems and email news on forthcoming
titles, readings, and poetry events.

☐ Please send me information on becoming a patron of Copper Canyon Press.

NAME: _____

ADDRESS: _____

CITY: _____ STATE: _____ ZIP: _____

EMAIL: _____

Copper Canyon Press
A nonprofit publisher dedicated to poetry

FROM The Second Book of the World,
   Which Is the Book of Relation

FROM The Second Book of the Book, Which Is the Body of the Beloved Which Is the World

Selected Books of the Beloved

PART ONE

FROM The Book of the Beloved and Us,
Which Is the Book of Eros

Even before speech
Revealed your secret,
There was looking.

Even before song
That gave you away,
There was gazing.

The beloved felt
Your eyes upon her;
He dimly understood
Why you looked at him
That way.
                    Speech
Of the eyes: the stare
And the glimpse.

The glance that lingers.

                    *

Her eye and my "I":
Her gazing
Creates me.

His voice and my
Ear—I'm seized
By hearing.

How because
Of the beloved
I come into being.

Under her touch,
All of me shudders.

*

The world looks
In all directions
Like that vase
Of chrysanthemums
On the table.
But the beloved
Looks only at you.

How easy to choose.

Yes, the flowers
Are beautiful

But the beloved's gaze
Makes you beautiful, too.

*

Hoarding your joys and despairs
As if they were clothes
You bought but never wore.

Look at this bright shirt:
A possibility you glimpsed
But feared to seize.

The beloved is waiting.
You have a date.
Put on that shirt before it fades.

*

It's all far too large
And various
For us to take in—

We'd burst
Apart if we tried.

Narrowed door
Of desire

That is
The beloved's body:

We'll enter
The world
Through her or him.

*

Sometimes the beloved's
Just a dance of glances,
Brief as a minnow-flash.

How grab that glimmer?
How seize that hint
With our clumsy fingers?

*

When we were young
We feared she
Would never come.

Even then we felt
His loss—felt it as lack,
As longing.

We never thought
How lucky we were
To have it all before us.

We dreamed the beloved's
Caress; we squirmed
And tossed in our beds,
Imagining pleasure.

*

There you were—stalling
For time,
Hoping the right words
Might arrive.
     Words
That could stop
Time in its flowing;
Some phrase to hold
The beloved
Against all going.

Curse of the shy—
Once more, that heart-cry
You ached to release
Muffled
To nothing but pulse-thump.

*

A smile on the face
Of the beloved,
And we caused it.

Never again having
To ask
The universe
If we have a purpose.

Settled forever:
The question of our worth.

*

"So, who will give
First,
And who
Will give most?"

My bold phrasing
Pleases me—
I think it proves
I'm in charge
And can sharply
Bargain
Over what
Parts I still control.

To my surprise,
He simply insists
I hold
Nothing back.

Her only request:
I surrender
All I possess.

*

With your embrace
You chose
Each other,
Which was
To choose death
And all that comes
Before it:
Sufferings
And joys
And infinite
Unintended harms.

Large choice
For such small arms.

*

And when the beloved
Is a person
So much the better,
So much the worse.

You'll know no peace.
Misery will be your pillow
And you will not sleep.

So much the better:
Staying up all night
Talking to her,
Thinking about him.

So much the worse:
Where is she now?
Where, in this wide world,
Is he wandering?

*

We could say
No to love,
But love itself
Doesn't say No.

We could say Yes,
Yet it might not
Arrive
Any faster.

Seldom responding
To our whims
Or commands,
The mysteries
Move
At their own pace.

Whole years go by
In which we never
Catch a glimpse,

And then suddenly . . .

*

Reciprocity—that's where
It starts.
        Not something
Given selflessly
Or grabbed without regard.

The free exchange—caress
Begetting caress. Gaze
Answering gaze.

                    Across
What gulfs, voice
Responding to voice,
As poem responds to poem.

                    *

If to say it once
And once only, then still
To say: Yes.

And say it complete,
Say it as if the word
Filled the whole moment
With its absolute saying.

Later for *but,*
Later for *if.*
                    Now
Only the single syllable
That is the beloved,
That is the world.

                    *

For such a journey
Maps are useless.

Physical distance—
The least of it.

Between one heart
And another—

A short road
And a long path.

Getting lost—
What's wrong with that?

*

To see the beloved,
To be seen by the beloved:
That's where being starts.

Looking with the eyes, of course.
But who could be filled
With such gazing and not
Want more?

Looking with words also.

Look and then leap.
Gaze and then speak.

*

Voice of the beloved
Searching me out,
Seeking me,
                Speaking me.

Speaking herself first;
Speaking his own being
In order to awaken mine.

*

The beloved insists
Even
We mollusks
Must frolic—

She's sent her bolt
To smash open
That
Thick shell
That was
My soul's abode.

And there's no more
Hiding, now
The core
Of me's exposed.

*

Extravagant catastrophe—
To be stunned
By wonder,
Destroyed by joy—

Blast and shatter;
Glitter and gone . . .

And so the heart
Must gather
All its atoms,
Glue them
With dew—

And so the world
Begins anew:
Miracle of molecules
Clinging,
The spider
In the dark night

Reweaving
Its torn web thread by thread.

*

Here's "anguish" and over
There is "dance."

Split the difference
And you have the heart
Trapped in the middle,

Turning on a spit,
Twisting on its spindle . . .

*

Lots of sorrow and a little joy.
Lots of joy and only a bit
Of sorrow.
                    Who can know
The formula beforehand?

We don't get to watch
As it's mixed. No one tells us
What's in it.
                    We lift it
To our lips—azure elixir
That burns our throats to crystal.

*

I dreamed she'd arrive by
Just sashaying in
Through my senses.

But for someone like me,
Love couldn't enter
Until
I was broken,
All the way to the center.

Right here, the blow fell—
A sledgehammer
Against a wall.
And so,
A ragged door
Was made,
And the beloved came to dwell.

                    *

The journey already so
Arduous
And uncertain,
Yet I've only reached
The surface
Of myself.
                    Exhausted.
Desperate
To rest awhile, yet
How much further
Beyond
The beloved beckons
With his otherness,
                    With her gesture
That promises
To reveal
What I need
To know:
Why it is I'm alive.

*

There's the daisy: white petals
And a plush yellow center.
And so we begin
Our anxious interrogation:
"She loves me,
She loves me not."
Plucking it bare
Like a plump chicken
We plan to cook.

Daisy comes from
"Day's eye"—the sun.
A flower as metaphor
For the world's splendor.

The beloved shining on us
All the time
And us with our silly questions.

*

Ask the tree or the house;
Ask the rose or the fire
Hydrant—everything's
Waiting for you to notice.
Everything's waiting for you
To wrap your heart around it.

That music has been playing
Since you were born.
You must be mad to resist it.
Always the beloved
Surrounds us,

Eager to dance.
All we have to do is ask.

*

Were we invited?
Was that what the beloved's
Smile signified?
Quick, say Yes.
Tell her we'll be there.
Tell him I can't wait.

I missed so many things
Because I was sleeping.
I don't want to miss this.

*

Bending over spring's first rose—
Only meaning
To breathe it briefly,
But its odor
Opens secret doors
Inside you, and you
Close your eyes
And press your nose
Deeper into its redolent folds.

*

Hold off, rain.
Of course, my garden
Craves water.

But the peonies
Are in full blossom.
If you fall now,
Their petals will
All be scattered.

Wait a day.
Let them feel
The pure joy
Of opening.

Fall tomorrow,
Then you can show them
Love
Is also a shattering.

*

To be alive!
Not just the carcass
But the spark.

That's crudely put, but . . .

If we're not supposed
To dance,
Why all this music?

*

When the world
For a single moment
Focuses on you,
You become the beloved.

Glowing. Almost unable
To contain your glee.

Precarious bliss,
It was for this, for this . . .

> *

Wanting it to last,
But
What's the chance?

We were made
To vanish.

One of
The things
We're best at.

Without a trace,
As if
We never lived.

And all we
Loved:
Dew on the grass.

> *

To loll in a sensual torpor—
That's fun for the young.

If we had not lost the beloved
We, too, would be lulled
By the body's pleasures;
We, too, would have despised

The songs of grief,
Which are the deepest
Songs of love, those
Low moans, close cousins
Of the quiet cries of lust
As it's gratified.

*

Loss and loss and more
Loss—that's what
The sea teaches.

The need to stay
Nimble
Against the suck
Of receding waves,
The sand
Disappearing
Under our feet.

Here, where sea
Meets shore:
The best of dancing floors.

FROM The Book of Loss and Grief

When we lost the beloved,
We lost the world.

A crack opened between
Us and all else.

Briefly, perhaps,
But how deep it was.
Who could forget
What was glimpsed there?

We stepped carefully across
Or leaped and hoped
We'd reach the other side.

But the chasm was real
And we were wordless,
Worldless,
And bereft of love.

*

There's no use in closing
Your eyes now—

After the lightning flash.

Isn't it already inside you:
Both wince and blinding?

*

Everything taken from us
At once,
And still we're here.

Standing still—maybe
At the edge of a great cliff
Only we can see;
Maybe that's why
We don't move
Though our blood does.

Stunned.
            Everything
Taken from us,
And we're still here.

*

Welcome to the kingdom
Of numb,
Where many
Live but none belong.

These are grief's
Thick
Transparent walls—

You can see through
Them,
But you can't feel.

Neither touched by
Nor
Able to touch.

Welcome to the kingdom
Of numb,

Where enduring
Is all
And flourishing
Is gone.

*

To die and yet
Live after—

How hide
That shatter?

What mask
Of bold
Or blank to wear?

*

Place the beloved last was—

An absence so dense
It might as well be presence—

Space scoured raw by flood.

*

To learn by heart
Is to learn by hurt—
Grief inscribing
Its wisdom
In the soft tissue.

Song you sing,
Poem you are—
Finger moving
Precise as
A phonograph needle
Along the groove of scar.

*

If the world were to end . . .

Yet it ends every day
For someone.
                 A death
Or sudden loss
And just like that
The merry-go-round stops,
Its cheery music ceases.

You climb off the horse
You were riding;
You leave
The painted lion behind.

You see it's dark now;
The park is closing
Or has already closed.

You follow a path
You hope leads out,

A path you never noticed before.

*

When the coffin was closed
And the lid screwed down,
When it was fed into
The furnace
And flames consumed it—
Your eyes were useless.

What tears could put out
That fire?
                And so
You shut them, let
The lids of your eyes
Close over the beloved's body.

For a while now—darkness.

And what you see will be inside you.

                *

Would I have withdrawn?
Would I have held back?

Would I have hidden
From the beloved,
Even for an hour
Or a minute,
If I had known
Our time
Would be so brief?

Only a single day?

Only a lifetime?

Only a world?

And now, it's taken away.

*

Not to make loss beautiful
But to make loss the place
Where beauty starts.
                        Where
The heart understands
For the first time
The nature of its journey.

Love, yes. The body
Of the beloved as the gift
Bestowed. But only
Temporarily.
                    Given freely,
But now to be earned.

Given without thought,
And now loss
Has made us thoughtful.

*

Growing
Through grieving,

Through
A deepening
We didn't choose.

*

To speak too soon
After such a wound—
What if it's only
A different bleeding?

Let the tongue sleep,
Your heart go numb.
Wait awhile in silence.

Don't even write.
Leave the page blank
As a wintry bandage—

Isn't that why snow falls,
So the field beneath it can heal?

*

Love without loss—
Hard to measure.
How can we test
Its depth?

Easy enough
To cherish
What's
Always there—
So easy
We forget to bother.

But what if
Love only starts
When the heart stops?

Stops, then
Begins again,
On the other side of loss.

*

What's over is over—

No sure way
To measure
Either
Grief or pleasure.

We'll never know
Whether
We took
More than we gave.

*

How easy to give up hope.
How easy to draw death over you
Like a black cloak. Cover
Your face, your eyes. Stand
There like a dead tree.
I did that, claiming it was penance,
Claiming I was sorry I was
Alive after the beloved died.

Who was I fooling? No one
Demanded I act that way,
Least of all the ones I loved
Who longed to live again
And could not unless I uttered
Their names, unless I told

Their stories, unless I felt
In my own bones
How much they loved the world.

*

We let death take him
Without a word of protest.
None of us spoke up—
Afraid to make a ruckus,
Afraid death might notice us.

We didn't dance or weep
Or scream our grief.
We let the beloved go
Without a song or poem,
And that diminished us.

*

Set beside the world's
Vast sufferings,
Our loss was small.

We know that.
And yet, for us,
It altered everything.

Taught us "much"
Is no measure.
Taught us depth is all.

*

When the awful
Happens,
The world
Pivots
And the rest
Is aftermath—

The hurt soul
Hides,
Huddles
In its hut
And lets
The heart
Harden until
It becomes
A stone rose
That only
Blossoms inward.

It knows one rule:
Survive, survive.

*

It wasn't death I discovered,

It was grief.
            It was living on
After the beloved was gone.

How awful it was and how easy—
All you had to do was breathe.

*

If deepest grief is hell,
When the animal self
Wants to lie down
In the dark and die also . . .

If deepest grief is hell,
Then the world returning
(Not soon, not easily)
Must be heaven.

The joke you laughed at
Must be heaven.
Or the funny thing
The cat did
At its food dish.

Whatever
Guides you back
To the world.

That dark so deep
The tiniest light
Will do.

*

"Sorrow makes us all
Children again," Emerson wrote
When his young son died—
"The wisest know nothing."

And grown Tennyson became
"An infant crying in the night;
An infant crying for the light,
And with no language

But a cry."
              Words
Written by those who were lost.

Given to us: paths in the dark.

                    *

When the beloved died
Our world
Was destroyed—
The one we made
By placing
Him or her at the center.

If we're patient and lucky,
We might enter
Another—
Beyond
What we knew or wanted:
One of risk and feeling,

One where nothing
Under us
Will ever again
Be steady,
And even to stand
We'll need to learn to dance.

                    *

I was asleep in uneasy
Bliss, and when I woke
The beloved was gone.

That's how life teaches us
We're born from loss.

Life taught me that
Without even trying,
Without lifting a finger.

To find the beloved
Again—now I have a purpose.

                *

That desolation is the door:
How be surprised at that?

All those moments we shared
Only prelude to this painful
Growing.
            Her loss forcing
It upon us, his absence insisting.

Not bliss. Never again bliss,
But maybe a deeper knowing.

                *

That T-shirt—it smells
Of him. Don't wash it.
I need to hold it
Close.
            I want to sleep
With it near my face.

How ridiculous this is:
Grief leading me by the nose.

*

Sorrow is good;
Tears are good.
But too much
Grief erodes.

What if all
The soft soil
Washes away
And only hard
Furrows remain?

Then what?

Then what can grow in us?

*

So many were given only
A dream of love,
So many given a glimpse
And that from such a distance.

Who am I to be ungrateful,
Who saw the beloved
Face-to-face?

*

The hug, the clutch,
The stranglehold—
Such are
The ways of love.

It seems the world
Is reluctant
To let go of me.

Nor do I
For my part
Wish
To release it
From my grip.

In and out
Of the agony;

Seldom or never surcease.

                    *

Autumn again. The leaves falling.

In one year, so many
Beloveds lost,
So many buried.
                    So many
Gone
From my sight forever,
So many become only songs.

Songs I can't sing yet,
Can't even bear to hear.

So many beloveds in one small year.

                    *

Not the loss alone
But also what comes after.
If it ended completely
At loss, the rest
Wouldn't matter.

But you go on.
And the world also.

And words, words
In a poem or song:
Aren't they a stream
On which your feelings
Float?
        Aren't they also
The banks of that stream
And you yourself the flowing?

          *

Maybe it's not the end
But only a pause
In our journey?

One step and then
Another.
One breath
Following the other.

As long as the poem
Proceeds
Word by word,
The beloved breathes.

To stop here, at the lip
Of the grave—
Whom would that save?

                    *

First, there was shatter.
Then, aftermath.

Only later and only slowly
We gathered words
Against our loss.

But last was not least,
Last was not least of these.

                    *

In the Navajo origin story
It began with weeping
And became a song.

"One of us was lost."

That's how it started.

It began as weeping
And turned into song.

And according to the Maori,
There's a way
Of grieving in which
A person's tears
Are matched
(Like rhymed couplets
In the West)

And words emerge
From these paired tears
Or merge with them—
They call it
"Weeping with meaning."

It's something only humans do.

*

Oh, I know: the beloved
Every time. Always the beloved.

But the beloved is gone.

We could lie down on the ground
And weep our lives away.
We could stamp our feet and refuse
Like little children.

And what would that accomplish?

Better to sing our sorrow song.

It's only words. But it's words
That bring the beloved back.

FROM The First Book of the Book

Part One: The Book of the Resurrection of the Beloved Imaged as the Story of Isis and Osiris

Resurrection of the body of the beloved,
Which is the world.
                    Which is the poem
Of the world, the poem of the body.

Mortal ourselves and filled with awe,
We gather the scattered limbs
Of Osiris.

            That he should live again.
That death not be oblivion.

                    *

The beloved is dead. Limbs
And all the body's
Miraculous parts
Scattered across Egypt,
Stained with dark mud.

We must find them, gather
Them together, bring them
Into a single place
As an anthologist might collect
All the poems that matter
Into a single book:

                    The Book
That is the body of the beloved
Which is the world.

                    *

Who wants to lose the world,
For all its tumult and suffering?
Who wants to leave the world,
For all its sorrow?

Not I.
And so I come to the Book
That is also the body
Of the beloved. And so
I come to the poem.
The poem is the world
Scattered by passion then
Gathered together again
So that we may have hope.

The shape of the Book
Is the door to the grave,
Is the shape of the stone
Closed over us, so that
We may know terror
Is what we pass through
To reach hope,
And courage
Is our necessary companion.

The shape of the Book
Is dark as death, yet every page
Is lit with hope, glows
With the light of the vital body.

        *

When I open the Book
I hear the poets whisper and weep,
Laugh and lament.

In a thousand languages
They say the same thing:
"We lived.

        The secret of life

Is love, which casts its wing
Over all suffering, which takes
In its arms the hurt child,
Which rises green from the fallen seed."

*

It's not magic; it isn't a trick.
Every breath is a resurrection.
And when we hear the poem
That is the world, when our eyes
Gaze at the beloved's body,
We're reborn in all the sacred parts
Of our own bodies:
                              The heart
Contracts, the brain
Releases its shower
Of sparks,
                    And the tear
Embarks on its pilgrimage
Down the cheek to meet
The smiling mouth.

*

Sadness is there, too.
All the sadness in the world.
Because the tide ebbs,
Because wild waves
Punish the shore
And the small lives lived there.
Because the body is scattered.
Because death is real
And sometimes death is not
Even the worst of it.

If sadness did not run
Like a river through the Book,
Why would we go there?
What would we drink?

*

Isis kneels on the banks
Of the Nile. She's assembling
The limbs of Osiris.
Her live limbs moving
Above his dead, moving
As if in a dance, her torso
Swaying, her long arms
Reaching out in a quiet
Constant motion.

And the river below her
Making its own motions,
Eddies and swirls, a burbling
Sound the current makes
As if a throat were being cleared,
As if the world were about to speak.

*

The poem is written on the body,
And the body is written on the poem.

The Book is written in the world,
And the world is written in the Book.

This is the reciprocity of love
That outwits death. Death looks
In one place and we're in the other.

Death looks there, but we are here.

                    *

Oh, there's blood enough,
And sap
From the stalks.
                    Tears, too.
A raindrop and the dark water
Of bogs.
                    It's a rich ink.
Indelible, invisible
(Hold the page
Up to the light,
Hold the page near a flame).

                    *

"What is life?"
                    When you first
Hear that question
It echoes in your skull
As if someone shouted
In an empty cave.

The same answer each time:
The resurrection of the body
Of the beloved, which is
The world.

Every poem different, but
Telling the same story.
And we've been gathering
Them in a book
Since writing began,
And before that as songs

Or poems people memorized
And recited aloud
When someone asked:

     "What is life?"

   *

The things that die
Do not die,
Or they die briefly
To be born again
In the Book.

Did you think
You would see
The loved one again
In this world
Or in some other?

No, that cannot happen.
But we have been
Gathering, all of us,
The scattered remnants
Of the beloved
Since the beginning.

In Egypt, the beloved
Is not in the pyramids
But in the poem
Carved in stone
Evoking the lover's lips
And eyes.
   In the igloo

The poem gathers
The dark hair of the beloved.

All the poems of the world
Have been gathering the beloved's
Body against your loss.
Read in the Book. Open
Your eyes and your heart;
Open your voice.
                    The beloved
Is there and was never lost.

                    *

I read the Book for years
And never understood a word.
Scrawled in its margins.
Wrote my own versions
Of what I read there,
But never got a thing right.

Didn't understand that each
Poem was a magic spell.
Was a voice,
And under that voice: an echo
That was the spell.

As if each poem clearly spoke
The word *Death*
And the echo said "Life."

Echo roiling the poem's surface
As the angel was said
To trouble the waters
Of Bethesda's pool in Jerusalem

So that the first person
To enter the water
After the angel had been there
Was healed.

                    *

You think I haven't known grief?
That I take it lightly? Don't know
How it gnaws your bones hollow
So you're afraid to stand up,
Afraid the lightest wind will
Knock you over, blow you away?

Maybe the wind is supposed
To blow right through you;
Maybe you're a tree in winter
And your poem translates
That cold wind into song.

                    *

I want to go back
To the beginning.
We all do.
                    I think:
Hurt won't be there.

But I'm wrong.
Where the water
Bubbles up
At the spring:
Isn't that a wound?

                    *

I saw my own body
Stiff and dead
Under a tree.
I saw the beloved
Bend over my corpse
And breathe life
In through my mouth.

And again I was alive
Inside.
       I felt my lips
Loosen and shape
The vowels of desire.
I knew I would rise
And walk in the fields.
I felt love move
Through my veins,
Felt it move through
All things in the world.

       *

What death shatters
(Sliver in the dirt,
Shard in the heart)

Song will find
No matter
How scattered.

Poem will gather
Into its pattern.

       *

No longer a part
Of the story,
Yet she's become
The story.

No longer a part
Of the world,
But he's become
The world.

Songs are forever
Saying this;
Poems knew this
From the start
Of time.
          They waited
Patiently in the Book
For that moment
When grief
Would open our ears,
When loss
Would open all of us.

*

To lose the loved one—
Is anything worse?
To die oneself—
Not desirable,
But far easier
Than living on past
The loss of the beloved.

So much of your heart
There in the grave.
And what comes in
To fill the emptiness?
Shame at being alive.
As if to survive means
You betrayed the beloved.

Then life is a penance
And tastes bitter.
You look at the dirt
At your feet; you
Never gaze at a face
Or lift your eyes
Toward the night sky.

You eat and talk and sleep
But you're really dead.
And all the time, the beloved
Is alive in the Book—
Waiting for you,
Eager to speak to you,
Eager to hear all the secrets
You've stored up in your grief
As if your body were a grave.

Eager to hear your voice.
Curious to know why
You withheld yourself,
Why you buried your love.

*

There's nothing occult going on:
It's not as if the skull opened
Along its ancient fissures
Like a bone lotus spreading
Its petals so as to let a blue
Light leak out.
                    Nothing
At all like that. No magic.
What happens is natural:
The heart uttering its hurt
And its happiness: syllables
Whose rhythm captures
The pulse of sorrow or joy,
The slow ache or throb of it.

And what occurs next can be
Explained by the physics of feeling,
By that science through which
Emotion becomes motion,
Love jolting the sleeper awake.

                    *

Can a river flow beside itself?
Can two bodies move together
Through time?
                    Or are they
Time itself: a liquid motion
Over stasis?
                    Some say Osiris
Was the Nile. And the banks
It overflowed. And the green
Stalks rising though the rich mud.

That the whole cycle of flood
And renewal was love.

*

Even the saddest poems have journeyed
Past death and been resurrected
As words on a page. Death never
Stopped the simplest poem. Death
Starts them, loss launches them out
Into the future, so they will someday
Wash ashore on the beautiful
Page of the Book: message scratched
On a log or lodged in a bottle:
"I write to you from the world."

*

Concentrating on those motions
That show hope most simply:
The hoe clearing the irrigation
Ditch so the water flows.
The green stalks poking up
Through the dark, Nilotic mud:
So many tongues uttering
Their joy.
   Or is it *our* joy
They utter? Who saw Osiris
Buried, his corpse swollen
And deformed by death.
Who wept above the spot
Where he lay a long time
In the earth, listening

To the whisper of worms.
And now it is spring
And the beloved returns:
Who was fat with death
Is slender as a sapling now.
And silent grief gives way—
We shout our joy as fields
Shout their green shoots.

In our despair we were as dead
As the earth in winter, dark
And inert. Now the world
Is reborn. Now the poem
Of the dead one
Comes alive in our hearts.

*

Love and loss, then life again—
The complete cycle.

As with the god Osiris—
Killed, then
Torn asunder, then
His remains
Sunk under waves.

Later, words like limbs
Gathered
Into the whole
Body of the poem,
Which is
The body of feeling.

What was destroyed
Is now reformed—
Rises up to float
On the water
Then lightly step ashore—

Like Botticelli's
Venus: resurrected, reborn.

Part Two: The Book of the Body of the Beloved
Imaged as a City Made of Poems

It would have erased everything human—
The deep snow of oblivion—
If those before us hadn't kept
Poking up
The huts of poems and songs.

And then: small houses
Huddled in a settlement.

And soon it became a village,
And next it was a town.

And now it makes its own weather.

Now the winds walk around it.
Now the clouds bow.

Now the snow recedes
And the Book of the beloved
Reveals itself as a shining city.

                    *

Some say Adam and Eve
Made it—
She from her praise,
He from his grief.

Some say they built it
Out of their
Fallenness—
He with his praise,
She from her grief.

Raising the walls,
Laying the roof;
She with her praise,
He with his grief—
Building the first house of song.

She with her grief,
He with his praise—
Making the holy human city,
Making the wholly human city.

*

If someone had said, when I was young,
That poems make life bearable
I wouldn't have believed them.

My world had closed in
On all sides.
I could hardly breathe.

If someone had told me then
That I would feel free . . .

A place where every poem
Is a house, and every house a poem.

When I first came here
Fifty years ago—the moment
I arrived I knew this city was my home.

*

Who needs plaques
Or nameplates when
The houses themselves
Are so distinctive?

Blake's cottage easy
To recognize
By the angels dancing
All day on the roof.

From the drain spouts
Of Baudelaire's villa
Gargoyles leer.

There's an orchid boat
Moored in the canal
Out back of Li Po's.

And Whitman's house
Is crowned with sod,
With grass deep-rooted
And swaying in the wind.

Dickinson's has two large
Windows on the second floor:
Staring, startled, intelligent eyes.

*

A thousand roads lead to it
And ten thousand paths.
Each reader finds it
In his or her own way.
Its gates are always open

Night and day.
                    Oldest
And newest city on earth—

Young poets creating
Almost impossible structures:
Tall, postmodern, made
Entirely of polycarbonate
Or Mylar.
                    While scholars
Digging into sandstone cliffs
Find pillars carved
With love poems in hieroglyphs.

                    *

Until I heard Neruda read his poems
Aloud, I never even knew
I could fly
To the city of poems.

He'd arrived that day by plane
For his first visit
To Manhattan, the city
Of Whitman, one of his heroes.

"*Vienes volando*," he intoned—
"You come flying"—
Refrain from an elegy
In which he summoned
His beloved's spirit over the Andes.

I stood in the crowded room
And remembered my own loved dead.

That was forty years ago, and yet
I can still hear his sonorous voice—
"*Vienes volando*"—
And whenever I hear it
I'm transported again to that other city.

(YM-YWHA Poetry Center, New York City, 1966)

*

Tang of salt in the walls
And boards
Of the house of the poem.

Not from harbor or shore
But the boundless sea
Of grief,
That ocean inside us.

Still, the maker didn't
Weep as she framed
Her song;
        He never
Paused to sob
As he laid out the flooring.

Born of sorrow,
Yet the joy in making it.

*

You're invited to visit
A particular poem—
To go often enough
To become familiar
With each of its rooms;
To nose around in the attic
And explore its cellar.

Encouraged to arrive early
And greet dawn
Through various windows;
To linger long enough
To watch the shadows
Arrive toward evening.

Only a guest, yet
Welcome to stay forever.
To stay as long as you want.
As long as it gives you pleasure.

*

There's only one river
That flows
Through the city,
But different poems
Call it different names.

In some it's Lethe,
River of oblivion;
In others it's Time
Itself—that stream
That moves through
All poems and laps

At the banks
Of words, slowly eroding.

Some name it after
A childhood brook
As if its current
Had moved alongside
Their own from birth,
As if they both emerged
From the same source.

Others dub it something
Exotic, as if to say:
You are a river no one
Has seen
Except in imagination—
You are the color
Of my longing
For the beloved,
Which is deep and pure.

*

So many brought here by water,
Though seldom a cruise ship or yacht.
Most in the small boat of self.

Some after long struggle—
Strenuously rowing upstream.
Others, tossed on the rocks
Or washed up half-dead on the shore.

*

Love overwhelms us.

Or death takes

One more
Of those
We cherish most.

Where else?

Where else can we go?

*

From a distance
The city of the Book
That is the body
Of the beloved
Glistens, as if marble
Were the only stone
Any poet ever used.

But when you get
Closer you see
It's coated with grime,
As if the whole city
Was built downwind
From Blake's
"Dark Satanic mills."

A good rain
Will always cleanse it.

Or even
A single tear
Falling on a single page.

*

Not everyone in the city
That is the Book
Of the beloved
Sleeps in a house—
Rimbaud, for instance,
Vagabonds about: a youth
With backpack, dog,
And homemade tattoos.
His poems are too
Restless to settle,
Appearing as phrases
Scrawled on walls—
Bold and disturbing,
Making us uneasy—
A sacred/demonic graffiti.

And Sappho, who's known
To the Book only
In fragments—it follows
Logically that she doesn't
Have a house—only a gown,
And that's in tatters:
Linen like gauze,
And where it's torn,
Revealing the body beneath—
Slender and passionate.
But don't pity her—
It's a garment that flatters.

Nor will Rumi permit a roof—
He won't have any barrier
Between the infinite and him.

You'll find him in a great
Open space, where he dances
On one foot, then the other.
You could say his house
Is the pillar of dust
His spinning raises up,
And he stands inside it, singing.

And Trakl each night after dark
Stumbles into the park
And clambers up into
The outstretched marble arms
Of an angel
And curls up in a ball.
Wadded poems stuffed
In his clothes will keep him
Warm.
                Angel of cocaine,
Angel of his suicide sister,
Angel of atonement—
Who knows, who knows?
He sleeps like a child
After a fever.
He sleeps as if all were forgiven.

                    *

Consider François Villon—
Murderer and thief
If half the rumors are true.
How did he come to live here
As if he were respectable?

My best guess, because he wrote
"*Où sont les neiges d'antan*"—
"Where are the snows
Of yesteryear"—a refrain
That followed a list
Of famous beauties he once knew.

I don't claim he was the first
To lament that bodily beauty
Vanishes like melting snow,
But when you think of the city,
Remember Villon.

*

Francis's "Canticle of the Creatures"—
It's a simple hut made of branches
And mud—he wouldn't
Have anything fancier.

"Brother Sun, Sister Moon"
Is how it begins—a poem
That's almost nothing
But a list of things he's turning
Into brothers and sisters—
"*Brother Wind, Sister Water.*"

So much love flowing out
But also streaming back in—
He's creating a giant family
With his wacky affiliations—
Like Whitman on an acid trip.

A poem that could have been
Written by a pagan,
Except he didn't write it at all
Because he was illiterate—
Couldn't read, couldn't write.
"Sister Tree, Brother Rock."

Wore a drab brown robe tied
With a rope. Tended
The poor, disturbed the Pope,
Who forbade him to preach.
He didn't really care—
People understood his message.

He loved to bellow the bawdy songs
Of the troubadours
As he wandered Italy's dusty roads
Without a nickel to call his own.

*

Whenever its enemies besiege it,
The city that is the Book
Transforms itself
Into heaps of scrolls
And huge twig-piles of words.

Whenever its enemies
Set it on fire
(A huge conflagration
That lights up the night sky),
They dance and exult,
Enjoying the blaze enormously.

And when the flames die down
They prod the embers
And feel proud of their power.

And before long, they're bored
And climb back on their high
Horses or jeeps and return
To their forts and towers.

They've hardly been gone an hour
When there it is again—that marvelous city.

                    *

White flag
Of the city—

No ensign
Of surrender

But radiant
Sign of desire:

Blank sheet
Of the page—

Bed with covers
Thrown back,

Ready
For the wars of love.

                    *

What's the Book after all but
One of the best watering holes
This side of paradise—

                  A place
Keats called the Mermaid Tavern.

He claims he was there and swears
It's full of poets "dead and gone"
Who drink and talk and sing
With those still living.

                     You'd think
They were a raucous crew, yet
According to him they seldom
Argue, preferring to keep
The ale flowing all night long
And on into dawn.

                 And if you believe
Keats (and I always do), the dawn itself
Never ceases, the dawn goes on forever—

And so they'll sing till the end of time,
Those poets in the Mermaid Tavern.

                *

Sometimes, entering
The house of a poem
You're greeted
By your other self—

That person you
Could have become
Had things gone
Differently.

                 Or even

Who you *really* are,
Though it's been kept
Secret, even from you.

Under the pretext
Of a guided tour
Your double
Tries to convey
An urgent message.

It's crucial but elusive,
Not found in the words
But in what you intuit
From hints and gestures.

It's something on which
Both your lives depend.

*

Today a letter arrived,
Sent from the city
Of poems—
The beloved
Summoning us.

The contents lucid,
The return address
Blurred by tears.

We must hurry there.
We must search
The city, high and low.

Even if it takes years.

*

The poems we love—what are they
Made of?
        Nothing.

Yet when we recite them
Our voice climbs the lines
As if they were stairs
Made of air
In a house made of breath.

Structure invisible as death:
A house made of breath,
Stairs
That are nothing but air—

Yet each so solid we can pause
When we want to and stand there.

       *

As I say aloud the opening line
Of my favorite poem,
My breath calms.
            Soon
The sounds I make
Set my hands dancing,
And next my feet
Begin to move.

Before I know it
I'm walking again

In the city.
My stride's jaunty,
My legs feel strong.

I'm an old man reborn,
Made young again
By the poems I love.

Reciting them as I saunter along.

FROM The First Book of Singing, Which Is the Book of Resurrection of the Beloved

Grief made you heavy,
So heavy you wanted
Only to lie on the ground.

And the Book you gripped
Despite its thousands
Of pages,
Was light, almost
Floated out of your hands.

You and the Book could
Easily have drifted apart—
It, rising into the clouds;
You, curling up in the dark.

But you held on. Something
(Maybe it was a single poem)
Told you not to let go.

*

Not many of them, it's true,
But certain poems
In an uncertain world—
The ones we cling to:

They bring us back
Always to the beloved
Whom we thought we'd lost.

As surely as if the words
Led her by the hand,
Brought him before us.

Certain poems
In an uncertain world.

*

Who'd even dispute
That we learn
First (and most)
By hurt?

But what we learn
Has no worth
Until words
Arrive
So the real work
Can begin:
              Singing
That transfigures,
Saying
That saves—
Lifting
The beloved

Out of the grave.

*

Who can measure the gratitude
Of the beloved?
To have lain so long in the dark
Listening to the worms whisper.
The eyes closed, the nerves numb.
And then to be brought alive.

And all because of you.
Because you sang the song
That someone wrote; or
Hummed it even, not remembering
The words but feeling the feeling of it.

*

An anthology gathered
Since the beginning of time,
Gathering itself.

Only to disperse as a tree
Scatters its leaves.
Only to tear itself apart
And give to each who needs.

*

Book of the beloved's resurrection:
Was and is and will be.
Holding all of history
In its arms.

Embracing also what's inside
Us:
    Reaching down
To our depths
And up to dizzying heights.

Extending outward to both
Horizons:
        Ocean in the east
Where the sun comes up
And in the west
Where it sets.
        And all
That's contained between:
What grows and moves
Or holds its peaceful place.

Occult power of the alphabet—
How it combines
And recombines into words
That resurrect the beloved
Every time.
                    Breaking open
The dry bones of each letter—
Seeking the secret of life
That must be hidden inside.

Grief will come to you.
Grip and cling all you want,
It makes no difference.

Catastrophe?
                    It's just waiting to happen.
Loss?
            You can be certain of it.

Flow and swirl of the world,
Carried along as if by a dark current.

All you can do is keep swimming;
All you can do is keep singing.

Letting go, when all you want is to hold.
Turning away, when all you want is to stay.

Almost all that's in the Book was written
On just such a day:

Someone remaining;
                    Someone going away.

Someone becoming silent;
                    Someone who must say.

                    *

You want
To get
To the bottom
Of it

But there
Is no
Bottom to loss.

On the sea of it
Loose
Words float.

Some cluster
Into
Rafts
Called poems.

                    *

Where is meaning
Found?
          Not
In the air

Nor in
The dark
Impacted ground.

It's in the song:

The one we sing
As we walk along.

                    *

Why should the grave be final?
Why should death be everything?
Isn't the world wonderful?
Don't we want more of it?
And in poems, life goes on
Forever.
                    Life and more life
Piled up in the Book.
Intensities and griefs
And pleasures accumulating
From centuries past, for centuries
To come.
And laughing at the notion
Of centuries, laughing
Not at time
But at the idea of finality.

                    *

Each of us standing at a particular
Spot we favor—our own location
Along the mortal shore.

Scanning the horizon.
                         There it is!
We watch the boat of the Book
Float by.
                    All our beloveds aboard.

Waving from the deck,
Calling out our name.
Some of them singing.
                    Some just
Gazing at us with that look we loved.

                    *

Weren't we more than
Electricity and dust?

Weren't we the hours
We lay beside
Each other?
                    Weren't we
The marks
We made on the page?

Weren't we the days
We knew we had purpose
And every step
We took was praise?

                    *

Knowing loss always wins;
Knowing nothing remains,
Nothing remains the same.

Knowing everything changes;
Everything dances away.

But setting your passion
Against passive vanishing.

*

Human heart—
That tender engine.

Love revs it;
Loss stalls it.

What can make it
Go again?

The poem, the poem.

*

Flipping pages randomly,
Or assiduously
Reading front to back—

As the religious
Search Scriptures
For the apt text,
The exact passage
That addresses
Their suffering
Or confusion,
So I search
Through books of poems.

When I find the right one
I'll know:
          Disturbed
And made easeful
In the same moment—

Hurt more deeply
By the blade that heals.

*

And if not you, then who?

Weren't you the one
Who cherished her,
Even from afar?

Weren't you the one
Who knew his worth,
Who knew the intensity
Of your love
Was not excessive?

How can you give up
The beloved as lost?

Always it was you:
The poems in the Book
Prove it.
      The songs
Attest to your passion.

*

Black marks
On paper
Or parchment,
Painted
On bark.
What magic
At work here?

Are these words?
Are these
A silent saying
Of all
We hold dear?

Are these proof
Of our being,

Of our being here?

                    *

Who says no lines are written
On the Book's blank pages?

Some have simply faded
And need to be written again.

But some are cries for love
So shrill no one can hear them,

Others inscribed with invisible ink
Because the secret's too painful.

                    *

The Book: cosmic jukebox
The size of the moon:

You can play as many
As you want for free.

If they're wrong
A thousand won't help.

If you choose right
A single poem will suffice.

                    *

No way they can bury
The beloved,
Even in the Book.

It's a tome, not a tomb.

All you've got to do
Is open it, recite
Those words aloud—

Bird that she is,
She's flying; he's flown.

                    *

And that's the gist of it:
Everything is risk—

The beloved lives,
Then dies,
Then (if we're lucky)
Rises again
Into the Book as song,

Or into the world
In some
Other form
Impossible to predict—

Simplest of stories;
Oldest of tales:

Sparrows sing it
From every hedge;

And swallows, also,
From their nests on the ledge.

*

There's no mystery
As to why
The Book's so huge.

To one reader
A certain poem
Is both
Beautiful and true;

To another, it's
Nothing
But platitudes.

If they start arguing
It will never end.
And who really knows?

What can we do
But put them
All in the Book?

Let each who reads, choose.

*

I never planned to die.
I never expected to be reborn.
I didn't give much thought
To anything, until
The Book let me know
The score. The Book
Did most of the talking.

"Where is your mother?"
The Book asked as if
I were a lost child.

"She's gone," I answered.

"How is it then I saw her
Inside me and talked with her,
As I talked with all the mothers,
Listened to all the fathers
Who spoke of their sons
And their daughters
And listened also
To the lonely ones
Who had no sons or daughters?"

All that between two covers?
In a book the size of a matchbox?
You have to open it.

If you want to see the light,
You have to strike the match.

*

Everything dies. Nothing dies.
That's the story of the Book.

If the Book was a bird
Those two sentences
Would be its wings.

Nothing dies. Everything dies.
If the Book was a fish
They would be its fins.

But the Book is the body
Of the beloved:
Two hands, two feet,
Two eyes.
        Lips to kiss.

      *

Can a poem do that?
Extract meaning
From grief?

Can the words
Squeeze it
Tightly enough
For a drop
To trickle out?

How will it
Taste
On our tongue?

      *

How lucky we are
That you can't sell
A poem, that it has
No value.
                    Might
As well
Give it away.

That poem you love
That saved your life,
Wasn't it given to you?

                    *

The mysteries we live among
Remain the same: love
And loss
And being a body in time.

Never was (or will be)
A shortage of passion.

Words in poems and songs—
Still our best hope
Of resurrecting
The body of the beloved,
Which is the world.

Book that stores them all:
How can it go out of fashion?

                    *

To feel, to feel, to feel.
Failing that, why live?
Might as well be a coffin
Drifting on a gray flood.

"The feel of not to feel it"—
That counts, too.
Anguish is one clear
Sign we're still here.

But we all need help.
The beloved's there,
And the world also.
And then there's the Book:

Poem after poem, song
Upon song. And all
With the same chorus:
"Wake up! You're alive!"

PART TWO

FROM The First Book of the World,
Which Is the Book of Changes

The world, the world—always
The world
Shining
Out there in the distance

How often I used words
To observe it

Used them as a lens
To bring it
Closer and into focus

But when the beloved died
Words failed

Or I did

And all I could do
Was lie down beside it in silence.

*

Who needs another earth?
This one would be
Heaven enough,
Emily D said,
If not for death.

But death is real, and all
That is
Flows toward its brink.

No wonder we need
Hope and courage—

What the Book brings.

To hold a pane of glass
Up to the world, to a part
Of the world: to see clearly
What's there and see it framed
In the shape of a page.

Can a poem do that? Be
Bald and alert as a photograph?
Who knows? The self is not
A clear lens. Emotions distort;
What we see appears closer
Or farther away, or warped.

And that's the truth of poems:
Both the wanting to lucidly see
And the warp of our passions,
And a third thing:
Discovering ourselves
Lightly reflected
In the glass we look through.

*

It's winter and I think of spring.
It's dark and I feel the light
That comes out of the body
Of the beloved, that fills
The room as it filled the life.

Alone in the dark you are
A body and the Book
Is another body, is the body
Of the other: the beloved
Who is the world.

Time isn't a door that only
Opens to shut;
Time isn't the lamp
That's on then clicks off.

Time is the great wheel of it,
Winter then spring; time
Is the great whirl of it:
The dance in which we hold
Close the body of the beloved,
Hold tight for dear life.

        *

It was so easy to love him then—
When we were young and he was
That body that roughly
Resembled our own.

We knew how to respond.

When he insisted: "Cherish me
Always," we hardly noticed
He didn't add: "And in this
Only shape."
              She demanded
It be forever
Yet never once claimed
The human would be
Her final form.
           Now
The beloved's become the world.

Now we must honor our difficult promise.

*

How many things
The beloved
Can become—
One after another
Or all at once.

We wanted love
To be easy:
"This bush, but
Not that tree."

Maybe both.

And also the bird
Flying between.

*

"Surprise me," the beloved said.

Command or enticement?
Flirtatious or earnest?

Tone of that voice
I no longer remember,
But I knew those words
Would rule my days.

As if the world itself spoke,
And I was supposed to answer.

*

It's time to turn the TV off
And listen.
                    That noise?
What is it?
Maybe it's only crickets.

Maybe it's distant music.
Maybe people
Are dancing somewhere
Not far from here,
The beloved among them.

Out into the street—
We need to investigate,
To find out what's there.

Even if it's only crickets.

                    *

Let's remake the world with words.
Not frivolously nor
To hide from what we fear,
But with a purpose.
                    Let's,
As Wordsworth said, remove
"The dust of custom" so things
Shine again, each object arrayed
In its robe of original light.

And then we'll see the world
As if for the first time,
As once we gazed at the beloved
Who was gazing at us.

*

How beautiful
The beloved.

Whether garbed
In mortal tatters
Or in her dress
Of everlastingness—

Moon broken
On the water
Or moon
Still whole
In the night sky.

*

Note to self: remember
What Emerson said
Of Thoreau—
That he loved the low
In nature:
            Muskrats
And crickets, suckers
And frogs.
            Not stars.

Songs of the carnal,
Songs of what we are.

*

Cat curled asleep
On my lap—
Beloved
As love-sponge.

Dog gazing up
From the floor—
All calm
And liquid eyes—
All fountain.

        *

Waking now, and we didn't even know
We'd been asleep in our luckiness.
A luckiness that now has ceased;
That the beloved's death
Has ended.
                Seeing the world
Differently, seeing it clearly
Or through a fog of grief,
But seeing it, where before
There had been no world,
Only the beloved blocking the light,
Only the beloved filling our sight.

        *

The hero who cuts a swath
Through enemy ranks
Armed with wrath—
I'm not him.
            Desire
Is all I have. And grief,
Perpetual companion

Of love.
　　　　Together,
We're a modest trio
Serenading the beloved
Who's shut herself up
In the Book
And won't come out.

Rage and sword
Won't open that door.
Pick that lock with a song.

　　　　　*

A pen's stronger
Than a sword.

Or the reverse,
For all I know:

People write
In what they love—

For some it's ink;
For others, blood.

　　　　　*

They're empty but swollen, Simone Weil said:
Words that begin with big letters.

She had in mind terms like *Truth*
And *Freedom*
As used by politicians
In speeches.
　　　　Squeeze them

She said—what oozes out
Is a mixture of tears and blood.

I suspect she's right, but
I'd add: that's not so
With a loved person—
Squeeze him or her
And it's called a hug;
There's a better
Than even chance
They'll reciprocate.
                    And not true
Of books of poems, either—
Full to overflowing
Those consoling fountains.

Bring your lips close—that liquid's not bitter.

                    *

Doesn't the soldier serve
The state? Isn't that his
Or her job? Doesn't
He dream of heroic deeds,
Or she of giving her life
To protect her family?

Whom does the poet serve?
The poet serves poetry
Whose form is the beloved,
Who asks not blood but love.

Soon the battle will begin.
Always, it's the eve of battle.
Do we have the courage we need?

The Book held close, the pages
You cherish clearly marked.
Will you be brave enough to speak?

*

The terror and thrill
Of battle, the fear
That has you shit yourself:
Has it come to this?

Someone's beloved
Become a corpse.
A flag on a coffin
Can't raise the dead.

Or suppose he comes back
Alive, with another body
Inside him that's not.

*

Invisible distance between
Yourself and the world:

Rage layered on the body
Like armor.
    Limbs
Thick with it, stiff,
Unable to move easily.

Unable to touch the body
Of the beloved because
Inches of it cover your skin.

*

When, in Valmiki's epic,
Bhima eats raw
The entrails of his enemy . . .

When Homer has Achilles
Burn young captives alive
On Patroclus's funeral pyre . . .

Let's call them what they
Are:
      Triumphs of rage,
Whose wine is blood;

Poems of the anti-beloved
In which *glory* rhymes
With *gore* and *war.*

Songs of death,
Shouted in a guttural chorus.

*

Soon enough, the gods will keep their nasty
Promise and Achilles's spear will pierce
Hector's chest.
            But now, for all its scars
And imperfections, his body is still whole
Beneath his wife's caress.
                It rests
On the floor—his helmet plumed
With a horsehair crest that, in battle,
Shakes wildly and makes him appear
Taller and fiercer than he really is.

Only a moment ago, as he took it off,
It scared his young son,
Who cried in terror
And ran from the room, never to see him again.

*

Lyric Revises the World

> *According to some, an army*
> *Marching or cavalry charging,*
> *Or a raiding fleet under sail,*
> *Is the loveliest sight*
> *On this black earth, but I say:*
> *Whatever one loves most is beautiful.*

Sappho, from fragment 16

Sappho, you started it all off
With your pithy remark:
"Whatever one loves most
Is beautiful."
                    Until you
Spoke up who knew
The personal
And passionate heart
Was what created value?

Who knew we *each*
Had power
To say what mattered?

All around you the guys
Jabbered on and on
About how awesome

Marching armies are,
How their hearts fluttered
When the cavalry charged.

But you had the nerve
To disagree
And insist on details
Both tender and specific—
What William Blake
Would later
Call the "bright particulars."

Not for you, those things
Hugely violent
That shook the earth
And only existed to hurt,
But rather what was intimate,
Personal, scaled to the human:

Your daughter, Kleis, "golden
As a flower,"
Or Anactoria, your lover—
The way her hips
Moved when she walked, her smile.

                    *

So obvious that the voice can cease
But the song doesn't stop.
That's why we have these marks
On the page.
                    If it were only
The palpable body before us,
If it were only the voice speaking,

It would be brief, would stop
When the breath stopped,
Would be a small, ephemeral thing.

But it isn't small. It's huge.
It has all of history in its shortest
Song.
          Empires rise and fall
In a couplet; fortresses tumble
Down and become owl-haunted
In a haiku's handful of syllables.

And empires aren't what matters,
Nor the ambitions of violent men.
Not according to this Book.
Not according to the beloved.

                    *

Grief today?
Joy's on its way.

Joy today?
Sorrow tomorrow.

                    *

Humid morning.
Last night's rain becomes
Sun-dapple on lawns.

Earthworm on the walk
Doing its slow dance
In honor of the world.

*

Hummingbird's furious
Hot heart
Beating without surcease.

How can those tiny wings
Cool it?
          The poem
Of the beloved—
Such intensity
It can hardly breathe.

*

The world comes into the poem.
The poem comes into the world.
Reciprocity—it all comes down
To that.
          As with lovers:
When it's right you can't say
Who is kissing whom.

*

Weighed down with the weight
Of the world. What can lift you?
And how did it become so heavy?
Is it because the beloved left?

How dark those rocks seem now.
That tree shadow more solid
Than the tree itself.
                    Help,
Help is on the way.

The beloved is coming.
A cloud over the sun
Doesn't mean there is no sun.

*

The grapes taste good.
I hope whoever grew
Them and picked them
Was paid well.

The poems in the Book:
Free as the air
They're made of.

What a business:
Praising the beloved.
What a business:
Loving the world.

*

The beloved moves through the world,
Is the world.
Becomes the hundred things we love
Or the one and only thing or person
We love.
        Shifting, restless,
Refusing to incarnate in a final form
As if to teach us to keep our eyes
Moving if we want to see the bird
Flitting from bush to tree:

There it is!
        No, there.
                No,

It's hidden now, you can't see it,
But you can hear its song.

       *

Whitman's list of the things he could see
As he sat, half-paralyzed,
An old man by a woodland pond.

The names of the different trees.
The birds he glimpsed or only heard
Yet recognized by their songs.

The bushes and grasses that grew there.

How happy those lists made him:
Red oak, hickory, poplar, larch . . .

Gazing from where he loafed
On the bank or from the pond itself
Where he floated naked
In the round pool of it:

As if he were the pupil
In a wide-open eye.

And the trees around it
Delicate and strong as lashes.

Oh, the world, the world,
What eye is wide enough?
What pupil sufficiently diligent?

Let's put our poems in the Book,
Let's add what we see to the beautiful list.

I know now the beloved
Has no fixed abode,
That each body
She inhabits
Is only a temporary
Home.
        That she
Casts off forms
As eagerly
As lovers shed clothes.

I accept that he's
Just passing through
That flower
Or that stone.

And yet, it makes
Me dizzy—
The way he hides
In the flow of it,
The way she shifts
In fluid motions,
Becoming other things.

I want to stop him—
If only briefly.
I want to lure her
To the surface
And catch her
In this net of words.

Where are you standing
That you can pluck
What you love
From the flood?

On the Book—more
Solid than any rock,
Rock being only
A slower flowing.

*

"Eternity" extends its seductive syllables,
But don't be fooled—

They have nothing to do
With you:
An embodied creature.

Nor does the beloved wish
To sleep a long time,
Much less die.

You know she won't
Even lie down
Except if it's for love.

And when he's gone
He's still alive
In all the poems he wrote.

That song of hers you sing:
Inside it she's tapping her foot in time.

*

Expected in one form,
Arriving in another—

But still the beloved.

                    *

We poets are always
Dipping our cups
In Heraclitus's river,
Drinking its health,
Toasting it with raised
Glasses.
            We know
A single drop of it
Sanctifies an entire
Gallon of wine.

We know it's the deep
Stream of the world
And surges through
Every page of the Book.

We know the beloved
Is an otter that dives
From its banks, frolics
In its swirling currents.

Or bows above its
Shallows as a heron,
Ready to seize
The minnow of us in her beak.

                    *

Might as well let go,
Might as well
Ease our bodies
Down into the flow.

After all, what part
Of the world
Do we really control—

We, who don't even
Know
What our own hearts hold?

*

We know the world's unstable—
That not even its atoms are tame.

We know the name of the game is Change
And even the game can change.

But can't the beloved stay as she is?
Can't he remain as he was?

Might as well tell the river
It has to return to its source.

Or else insist to the candle
It mustn't melt from its flame.

Only fools lament the rules
When they've always been the same.

This may not be what we came for,
But this is where we came.

*

"Why not a brief respite?"
I plead with the beloved.

"Bad idea," she insists:
"There's a world out there
You need to see, to be."

"But I'm tired," I whine.

"Sorry," the beloved
Responds, "you'll rest
When you're done.
Meanwhile, there's a word
In here" (she's pointing
Toward her heart)
"You need to become."

*

If you believe Shakespeare's
Sonnet, the beloved's
"An ever-fixed mark"—
A still star ships can steer by,
Something unwavering.

To me the beloved's more
Like that Chinese fable
Where a man boarded
An empty raft floating by
And was swept downstream
To the sea and from there up
Into the River of Heaven.

And even aloft, in final
Star-form, he didn't stay
In a single spot but
Wandered.
                  And still
Wanders, following his own heart.

                  *

Yearning for permanence, and who wouldn't?
Longing to believe it will last forever,
But what does? Nothing I know of.

Even the things that seem to stand still
Flow slowly into other forms.

The beloved's first and only lesson:
Everything that is, becomes.

FROM The Book of Questions, Which Is
Also the Book of Suffering

Well of course you could think
Of a poem as a wound:
Life leaking out.
                    Loss
Could feel that way; often does.
The beloved here and then gone,
Leaving a gaping hole in the air.

But isn't it also an opening?
Doesn't the world come pouring through?

                    *

Last night, a huge storm.
Branches torn from the maple,
Plants overturned on the porch,
Spilled from their safe little world,
Their clay pot with its gallon of dirt.

And won't there be worse?
Won't it happen to the people
We love? Then we'll know sorrow.

The branch can't be put back
On the tree. We scoop up
The earth and cover the roots—
Who knows whether it will live?

                    *

Traveling, you begin to long
For home;
                    Settled in one place,
You get bored and antsy
And dream of hitting the road.

And weren't they restless
Even in paradise, even
In Eden?
            Trying this
And trying that—who knows
What will make you happy?

                        *

So many to choose from,
But some are just words.

Couldn't the beloved tell us
In which poem she's hiding?

Couldn't he hint at where
He's concealed himself?

Must I read everything?
Must I search years?

Why not? Why not?
Easily found, easily forgot.

                        *

The motions so cautious,
Gestures almost not worth
Making.
            Do you think
The beloved rewards this?
Have you never heard
Of extravagance?
                        Love
Parceled out bit by bit
So it will last longer.

Look at the beloved—
Can't you see her laughing?

*

Beloved—word
That is
A world;
World inside a word.

What if it hadn't been?
What if it hadn't been heard?

*

Your Yes against all those
Shouted noes.

How brave you were.
What courage it took.

As if a single self defied
The whole cosmos.

So what if it all took place
Silently inside you?

*

Sometimes only a groan emerges,
Or an almost shapeless cry.

Our grief defeats us.
Words won't come.

We must lie down in the dust awhile.

Bitterest of all—
The beloved
Turning away
From us
And with that
Turning, taking
Away the world.

Calling the world
Back—one
Word at a time—
Out of the abyss
We have become.

Someone else called out
To the beloved
And we were jealous.
She turned her head,
As if she heard a voice;
His face went suddenly
Vague and faraway.

Then anger came over us.
We ourselves could have
Destroyed the beloved;
Could have wrecked
The world in our rage.

Had the lesson ended there
We would have been humbled
And left alone in the void

Of death.
          But everything
Passes. The passion swept
Over us like a huge wave:
We were lifted and tossed down.
But we did not drown.

                    *

Locked in your body
As if in a shrine:

Trying to hide
The beloved inside you.

Never alive—
Not the same as never died.

                    *

How is it, by dusk
I'm nothing
But husk
And stumble home
With all
The grace
Of a walking coffin,

Who only this morning
Strode down
The sidewalk—

An upright "I,"
An animated pronoun
Alive

With the thrill
Of being
A being inside my skin?

*

Something you never even
Knew you loved,
And now you've lost it
And you're grieving.

Where is the end
Of mysteries?

Lighter and lighter
As we grow older;
As we cast stuff off
Or stuff gets lost.

Lighter and lighter,
And still it's dark inside us.

*

Trying hard just to listen and let
The beloved's story enter,
Though I'm tempted
To turn away

Or to use my own words
To put a wall between us.

Eager to reassure quickly,
As if compassion
Could save me
From my own fear.

How my ears burn
With the blush
Of what she confesses,

Or go cold and bloodless
As he tells of all he endured.

*

There are questions
That must be asked
But no one alive
Can answer,
And yours is one of them:

Where,
You want to know,
Was the beloved
Then?

When, in the dark
Orchard, he hurt you.

When you curled up
In the tiniest ball
A child's body can be
And still the blows fell.

*

Hunkered down,
Nerve-numb
In the carnal hut,
The cave of self,
While outside a storm

Rages.
      Huddled there,
Rubbing together
White sticks
Of your own ribs,
Praying for sparks
In that dark
Where tinder is heart,
Where tender is not.

         *

Scar they stare at.
Star they're scared of.

Mark of the beloved—
A brightness that frightens.

To be touched so:
Taken past harm
To the place poems know.

         *

Sometimes we write
With our blood—
It's that intense.

Or ink flows freely
From our pen
As if from a wound.

Then the page is a body
And the body's a page

And a voice calls us:
Write this down, it says.

*

Remember Jacob and the angry angel
Who assaulted him? That fight
Was no one's idea of a joke.
And it can happen (who knows why?)—
The world suddenly deciding to crush you.

All night you struggle for your life,
And then it's dawn and somehow
You've survived.
                    But what if the worst
Were still to come?
What if you felt your heart
Slowly filling with a bitter wisdom
Blended of tears, rage, fear, and shame?

Now what cup? What cup will you drink from?

*

Some of us unlucky
In love—
Choosing poorly,
Or ourselves
Never even
Chosen at all.

For us, the Book
Has assembled
Laments—
Songs that express
Our sorrow and rage.

*

Those who wake in the middle
Of the night read a different Book.
For one thing, the world's all dark
Around them as if it disappeared.

The poems they read are anxious,
As if they feared the world
Might not return next morning
Or, if it did, might bring them
Sorrow or bad news. More sorrow,
More bad news.
                    A little light
On the Book's white pages
While they read for an hour:
Pages lit up like a sail at dawn.

The boat alone on the sea
But the wind steady, pulling them along.

*

Rain last night.
Leaves in the street.
I look up.
                The tree
Is full; not a sign
That a single
Leaf is missing.

Poem in the Book
That seems a lie,
That offends
Your suffering:

Tear it out,
Throw it away.
No harm done.

Tear them all out—
Grief can be that deep.
They'll return
When the time's right.

*

Could it all be said in a single poem
And not be completely cryptic?
There's Issa's haiku about
His daughter's death:

"This world of dew
Is only a world of dew.
And yet, ah, and yet . . ."

How the two lines seem to accept
That life's ephemeral,
And then that last:
A cry of quiet anguish.

Accept, but protest. Yield,
Then resist.
                The heart
Would have it both ways.
To see the world and say it true
Means starting with loss.
But that's not what the heart wants,
That's not where the singing stops.

*

Shattered?
        Of course
That matters.
          But
What comes next
Is all
I can hope to master.

Knowing, deep in my
Bones,
Not all hurt harms—

My wounds?
         If
I grow
Through them
Aren't they also a boon?

And doesn't disaster
Sometimes
Mask the arrival of grace?

        *

What suffering! Why isn't
The earth covered with tears
To the very mountain peaks?

Ah, but it is and always has been.
And the globe is filled
To bursting with groans.

And above it all the Book
Floats like an ark.

Not serene, but separate
From all the agony.
Not indifferent but other,
Like the beloved.

If you can glimpse it
Among the waves, swim toward it.

*

Weeping, weeping, weeping.
No wonder the oceans are full;
No wonder the seas are rising.

It's not the beloved's fault.
Dying is part of the story.
It's not your fault either:
Tears are also.
           But
You can't read when you're
Crying. Sobbing, you won't
Hear the song that resurrects
The body of the beloved.

Why not rest awhile? If weeping
Is one of the world's tasks,
It doesn't lack adherents.

Someone will take your place;
Someone will weep for you.

*

To add our own suffering
To the world's: tempting
When we're young,
Easy to confuse that
With love.
                    As if
The beloved desired
Our sacrifice, wanted
Us to be the moth
Impaling itself
On the candle's radiant
Thorn.
                We'd only
Smother the flame.

What the beloved wants
Is to burn more brightly,
To have more life.

FROM The Book of Searching, Which Is
the Book of Risk

All those years
I only had to say
Yes.

      But I couldn't.

Finally I said Maybe
But even then
I was filled with dread.

I wanted to step carefully.
I didn't want to leap.

What if the beloved
Didn't catch me?
What if the world
Disappeared beneath my feet?

       *

And isn't the world
Endless risk?
Does it make any
Difference
When I forbid
The beloved
To go?
When I demand
The world
Be stable and safe?

As if "a bird had stamped
Her foot," said Emily.

As if the air cared.

*

To open the Book
Is to open yourself.

But to close it—
That's not so easy.

Once you know
The beloved is there
And not lost forever . . .

Once you've felt
All those feelings again . . .

Closing the Book—
It can be done.

But to close yourself?

*

What was it the beloved
Promised—out of
His infinite passion,
Out of his deepest love?

Whatever it was,
Eternity had no part in it.

Sometimes only the length
Of a single poem;

Sometimes just a few
Words of a song
Disturbing the air—
And then she's gone.

*

Ashes and charred sticks
Of the extinct campfire,
The poet searching
For any trace of the beloved—

Always the same scene opens
Those pre-Islamic odes

Needing only the smallest
Proof of her existence,
Of his having been there—

Enough to give the poet
Hope as she returns
To the desert, as he
Begins the journey of his poem.

*

The lost beloved speaks
So softly,
Less than a whisper

Except in dreams
Where we've even
Had long conversations.

But in dreams I'm
Never sure
It's really him or her—

Really *that* particular
Person.

And when I'm awake
How can I know
Who is addressing me?

Voice so soft
It could be my own thoughts.

*

Throwing away hope—knowing
I only used it to offset
The night's despair.

Giving up words.
After all, they reveal
Just so much, but
Look at all they conceal.

Accepting that my groans
Are part of my growing.

Wading naked into the day.

*

From bliss to abyss—
One quick slip.

Ditto for kiss
To chasm.

Same with
Rapture
To fracture.

All joy leads
To disaster.

What matters
Is what comes after.

         *

And it happens, of course:
Harm comes to the beloved.

We must be brave
Even if we don't feel it.
She needs us. He has
No other ally.
Act now. Later for questions
And uncertainty;
Later for fear and second-guessing.

To risk all for the beloved—
How else will we be saved?

         *

Why not admit terror's
At the heart of it?

The constant fact
We could lose
All we have;
Not just the beloved
But everything
We own
And our health, too.

What would be left?

The world, yes, but
The world going
About its business,
Deeply indifferent to us.

Would a song come then,
When we had
Nothing?
                    A song
Made
From our emptiness
Shaped into words,

Made of nothing
But the air we breathe?

                    *

It's narrow, and no room
For error—I zig

And zag through
The treacherous channel.

What fool said joy
Is less risky than grief?

My ship could wreck
On either shore.

Needing to navigate
By contradiction:

What I want to grip
I need to release.

When despair says
"Let go," I must hold.

*

Timorous me—
Wanting
The heart
But not
The hurt.

Insistent
Beloved:
"That's not
How it works."

*

Not hoping for ghosts
Or other worlds;
Hoping for something
More full-hearted
And passionate—
Hoping the beloved
Laughs at death,
Brushes desolation aside
Like a veil or web.

Hoping poems summon
Him, songs bring her
Back.
        Hoping when
My pulse quickens
It's a sign
The beloved's alive inside me.

*

The beloved is in the Book,
And so is the world.
They've become one
With the word.

So all risk is over then—
Everything's
Safe between covers?

Now we can pretend
The Book's
A bed and go
To sleep
For a long time
With a blanket
Pulled over our heads?

Not so fast. Open
The Book
And it opens you.

After the first song
Sinks its teeth
In your heart,
You have to start over again.

*

Who'd want to be
That plaster statue
Of the god Calm
Around whom
Chaos
Swirls and swarms?

Better to swim
Through harm
Than ride
So high above it
That we look
Down on suffering.

You must descend,
Love said,
You must embrace
What seeks to break you.

*

Sometimes, reading the Book
Is our way of sending a cry
Across the abyss
Loss has opened inside us.

And in certain rare moments
What we find there
Is like an answering kiss.

But (why lie?) mostly
The world's a grim place;
And sometimes it's
Deeply cruel.
                    Still
This much is true:
When you say No,
All you get is loss and death.

If you say Yes, who knows?

*

When we're young there's lots
We don't know about
The beloved:
How he or she is only housed
Briefly in this or that body.

Mostly, the beloved is the world—
But we're not ready to see
That yet, not able to bear
The idea that the beloved
Won't necessarily gaze back at us
With eyes like ours, won't
Wrap us in his or her arms.

We want risk, but comfort, too,
Comfort most of all.
We're still clinging to our loneliness,
Not yet ready to be alone.

*

Well, it can't be helped.
Much that's essential
Has been decided
By powers far greater
Than ours.
                    What we
Can do is limited,
But now
We must respond.

Things seem grim—
Listening, you'd think:
Sounds like defeat
From here on in.

But what if it's also
An invitation—
An invitation to sing?

*

I ransacked the world
Around me,
But she'd
Become words.

I pored over books
Of poems,
But he'd
Become a person.

Years with nothing
But hints
And glimpses,
Yet the odds—
Not impossible:

The beloved's
Searching for me
Even as I search for him.

*

Comes in all shapes
And sizes.

Always eager
To surprise us—

The beloved
Appearing

In a thousand
Guises and disguises.

Perhaps that cat,
Pausing

In the doorway
To lick its paw.

Or surely, that dog . . .

*

Two things poems
Teach:

Death of the body—
Best accept it.

Death of the heart—
Better not.

*

Written in a distant
Country,
Addressed
To someone
Long since dead—

Improbable journey
By which
It's arrived here
And found me

To whom it now
Speaks quietly,
As if I,
And I alone,
Were always intended.

*

Why are we so scared of it—
"The burden
Of the mystery"?

The beloved—she's
Carried it
In poems
Whole centuries
Before we were born.

He'll be lugging it
In songs
Long after we're gone.

Not slavishly weighed
Down with it—
More the opposite:

When all is said and done,
Who could be crushed by love?

*

Relying on a map?

We're already
Half-trapped.

Guided by song?

Finding
Ourselves
As we travel along.

> *

One thing's for sure:
Our journey
Takes place
As much
In the silence
As in the spoken.

The poem itself
A village at night;
Its words:
A cluster
Of shuttered huts.

The path we're on
Goes past them and beyond.

> *

This room crowded
With memories, even this
Must be emptied.

Let it go. Let it all
Go. We must make
Space for the beloved's
Return.
            Nothing here
Is precious, nothing
We can't live without.

Or if there is, let it go
And the beloved
Will bring it again
When she returns.

Let it go, now.
Even this must be emptied.

*

Clearing out the room
That had been a shrine
To the beloved.

Now it all seems junk.
Now we must empty
That space, perhaps
Even paint the walls
A new, bright color.

Be brave. Admit it:
All this dusty stuff
Needs to be tossed
In a box and hauled
To a dump.
It's morbid.
It shows a lack of faith.

The beloved was never
These inert objects.
The beloved was alive.

As she is now inside you,
As he is now in the Book.

*

Closing my fists,
Tightening
My grip,
Sealing my lips.

Acting as if
By holding
Something back
I'll get to keep it.

It was never so.
Let go, let go.

Each kiss
You give
Could be the last.

Bestow, bestow.

*

To Guillaume Apollinaire, the beloved
Was "la jolie rousse"—"the pretty
redhead."
          He fought in World War I
And was seriously wounded.
But his beloved's red hair
Was not the color of war or blood,
It was the radiant color of love.

To him, the beloved was adventure:
Her red hair a flag in the distance,

Rallying him, commanding him
To venture forward into the unknown.

He followed her.
He left behind his books, his poem.

PART THREE

FROM The Book of the Body of the Beloved,
Which Is Also the Second Book of Singing

That ancient Egyptian poem
Carved on a pillar—
In it, she's showing her lover
A pink minnow
She caught
In her cupped hands

Yes, she's aware the water's
Turned her
Linen dress transparent

Scene from a poem
Composed three
Thousand years ago—

It's all just sand and dust
Now
And a few stones
Carved with hieroglyphs
But look—
        There they are:
That little fish and the two
Lovers standing close
To each other

Waist-deep
In a quiet part of the stream

       *

This is my ode to *O*—

Vowel so empty,
Vowel so full.

This is my ode
To the body—

House made of
Flesh and moan

Whose every
Orifice is holy—

O is the door
We go through—

So small, so small

Yet the room
We enter—immense.

*

Most poems
From mouth
And tongue,
This one
From teeth:
Playful nip
On your thigh.

Hours later
It still hurts;
Next day,
A bruise,
Tender
To the touch.

Whenever
You rub it
You think of her.

If a peach leads you into the world,
Into an appreciation of its delights,
How much more so the beloved.

A morsel of peach meat, a single
Kiss and you know pleasure
Has depths beyond measuring.

All this not subject to loss but
Certain of it—guaranteed
To vanish.
        Therefore more precious
Therefore brought back
By poems and songs. The mouth
Open as if to sing, as if to sink
Its brave teeth in a peach.

        *

There's a long-ago scene I like
To imagine
Though I know it never
Happened:
        She's asleep
Now in the small room
They share.
        Keats
Is still awake
At his desk
Feverishly
Trying to translate
Her body into words—

Those ripening breasts—
Their "soft fall and swell."

He pauses, puts hand
To chin and stares
Off into space—
A pose
He's perfected
For working on poems.

After a bit, he's restless
And stands up
To cross the room,
Bend down, and
With his lips,
Closely follow the original text.

*

Si je t'aime, prends garde à toi!
Sings Carmen in Bizet's opera:
"If I love you, watch out!"

Good advice: she's dangerous.
Love is dangerous.
                      As is the world.
It isn't only loss—there's lots
Of weird malice loose on the planet.

Of course her song is in the Book,
Not as a warning but an invitation:

"Welcome," it says, "but be alert."

*

Some of us, when we're young,
Can't get enough of poems
About sex and death—

We're convinced they'll instruct
Us what to expect when
Those two mysteries finally arrive.

No one tells us even the best maps
Often just guess what's next.

No one says: "Old mysteries are
Always new
When they finally happen to you."

She unbuttons her cotton blouse;
The car coming toward you
Begins its slow slide
Across the black ice.

There you are.

To warn or advise—equally useless.

                    *

Certain poems, because of their vowels,

Have the power to arouse
The soul from its torpor and cause
It to rise:
            Moans and sighs
That become bright threads
Of the fabric the beloved weaves

By firelight, something
(As the hymn to Aphrodite goes)

"More golden and lovely than life itself."

*

Going and coming, but
Also lingering.

First, it was
The beloved's turn,
Then yours.

Yet you both
Arrive
At the same place—

A quiet space
No bigger
Than a smile

You find inside you
When the throbbing stops.

*

Bald, high-domed Taoist sage
Holding the Peach of Immortality
In one hand, a hiking staff in the other.

I like to think he's reciting a poem,
One that begins: "To eat a peach . . ."
One that stresses its succulence

And how the sticky, delicious juice
Dribbles down your chin.

He's fresh from a rendezvous
With the beloved. Peach
And poem—both are her tokens.

                    *

Autumn with its too-muchness,
Stretching the boundaries
Of song.
                    The grape
Ripe against its skin—
One more day of sun
And it will burst with joy.

One more day under the beloved's
Gaze, the beloved's sway,
And we will die of love.

                    *

According to the Big Bopper
In the immortal "Chantilly
Lace," a wiggle
In the walk is one ingredient
That makes the world
Go round.
                    Something
Sappho also noted
Twenty-six centuries ago
When she watched Anactoria's
Hips shift as she strolled

And wrote: "Whatever
One loves most is beautiful."

Book so full of wisdom,
Stuffed with it. Crammed
With astute observations
About anatomy in action!

*

Ordinarily so mild, but suppose
The wrong song
Releases
All he keeps
Locked inside?
Or a poem frees
What she's concealed?

Exploring a poem's
Dark corridors,
He might
Meet his double.
Humming that tune,
She could uncover
Her secret self.

Next, she might open
Her mouth wide
And allow
Her tongue
To wag as wild as it wills.

Or he could start howling
At lung-top,

Letting loose
All that's rude and foolish.

So what? So what?
Why must the beloved always be sober?

                    *

Some poems offer escape—
They're floating islands
Anchored only
By a cloud-rope of words
We can climb.
                    Some
Are the opposite:
Insisting on
Embodiment—
As if they were tattooed
On the beloved's thigh.

Still others are short
And sharp—arrows
Aimed
Straight at our
Target heart
As if the purpose
Of beauty
Is to hurt us more alive.

                    *

Loving those poets most
Who couldn't read
The simplest maps

Who stumbled
At every step they took

Whose poems show me
Bruises
Teach more than books.

*

Praising all creation, praising the world—
That's our job: to keep
The sweet machine of it
Running as smoothly as it can.

With words repairing where it wears out,
Where it breaks down.

With songs and poems keeping it going.
With whispered endearments greasing its gears.

*

"Audacity of Bliss"—that's what
Emily Dickinson called it.

More than once I've felt it
And knew if I could
Turn it into words and share it
I'd have a reason to live
And no matter
How badly
Life turned out I could bear it.

I cherish that night she woke me
To hear her recite:

"Before and After—Vanished—
There is only—Now.

A Kiss—Appropriate
On its shining Brow."

Who only a year earlier
Had appeared in another
Dream to announce:
"We are bound by words
And wonder to the world."

Then she scowled and smiled
At the same time
And told me to write it down.

Who was I to disagree?

*

Dancing to her song
From the day I was born.

More and more proper
As I grew older.

Now, I'm downright
Solemn as I plod along.

You'd never know
I was anything but sober,

Yet deep inside me—
Still grooving to that tune.

*

Easy to gaze at stars,
Harder to stare at scars.

The beloved up close—
Even her hurts are holy.

*

"Astonied, stark in
Amaze they stand"
Goes the refrain
From a love poem
Thomas Campion wrote
So long ago its English
Is something
We barely understand:

Astonied then meant
"Turned to stone"
But it was on its way
To becoming *astonished.*

On its way to praising the beloved.

*

Here it is: a room chock-full
Of late-Greek statues,
Many of them naked
And with certain parts
Of their anatomies
Polished to a high sheen
By passing hands
As the centuries passed.

Can't help but recall
Plato's contempt for all
Art based
On a body's curves—
He preferred geometry,
Its abstract forms so "pure,"
So "free from the itch of desire."

Yet the rest of us, down
Through the centuries,
Voted with our hands
By running a palm across
Apollo's marble buttocks,
Or cupping Aphrodite's bust.

Gestures crude and foolish, yes—
But how brightly
Those ideals shine
That were so lovingly rubbed.

*

Could be I'm just outside
Eden—a desolate place
Blank as a white page

But as soon as lust
Rubs together
Two words—
I and *she*—
We'll start
To people this space.

How the long bone
Of the personal

Pronoun
Warms its cold
Length against her fur!

Friction of their contact
Doesn't hurt,
Gives birth to other words.

*

It's pretty much a consensus
Among us poets:

What we humans have
In common
Are our senses.

And only an idiot
Would dispute
That they're our
Greatest source of joy.

Embodied, mortal:
What we are,
What everything we love is.

And so, grief enters
Through the portals of bliss.

*

Jaw-drop when I first
Saw her—
Called that *awe.*

Then she spoke
Directly to me
And my cheeks
Flamed
With unworthiness—
That was *shame.*

And so, between
Those
Two extremes
It all began:

The long dance
That cries out to be named.

*

Desire in the vowels,
Rising
From our open throats.

Courage in consonants,
Thick as sinew
That our teeth bite into.

*

If words had lips
They'd
Kiss things.

If fingers,
They'd caress;
If arms,
They'd give
Fervent hugs.

If bodies,
They'd rub
And nuzzle
Against
One another.

I don't know
About
The world,
But words
Were made for love.

*

Often, there's nothing
Between me
And the abyss
But a single kiss,

And yet what a pair
Of lips can do!

Whispering sweet
Nothings in her
Secret ear;
Or how her mouth
Honors
A drooped part,
Giving it heart.

Reciprocity: pretty
Word for what
We do
For each other—
Shared spasms
Bridging deep chasms.

All testimony I know shows
That when we go
We'll each go
Alone.
      Luckily
We sometimes come together.

       *

Watching as words leap
The gap
Like spark or spasm.

Or flow smoothly
Over the surface
Of our fingers
To pool briefly
In songs and poems.

Some mixture of us
And the beloved.

Some elixir.

Some mystery
We've come here to witness.

       *

Suppose you could evoke
The entire body of the beloved
In a single poem.
Would it be all nouns?
All verbs?
      Would it

Contain the word *I*?
Or would that pronoun be
"Understood" as in Chinese
Poems where it seldom occurs
Since it's known to preside
At the center of all things,
Present by its absence,
Absent as a presence?

Which makes it resemble
The body of the beloved
Called back from oblivion
By all the poems in the Book.

*

Not all poems seek
Permanence

Some of them ephemeral
As snowflakes
In your open palm

Think of those
Lovers' couplets
That wove tall
Meadow grass
Into an afternoon's bower

Some forever

Others just one sweet hour

*

That song—why would it be
Stored in a college library
Or locked
In some dusty archive
Where it would only molder
And be nibbled
By bugs?
       I saw the poet
Hand it
Directly to the beloved—

She has it in her keeping;
He never lets it out of his sight.

It's there on every jukebox—
You could play it yourself tonight.

        *

Little fish of feeling, small
As the beloved's toes;
Little nibblers like erotic
Shivers.
       Caught in the net
And hauled up on deck—
Spilled in a silver heap in your lap.

Weaves a net wide as the sky,
Yet able to catch the tiniest fish—
How does the Book do that?

       *

Bittersweet, bittersweet—

Sappho's word. She made it
Up—the complex taste
Of love.
        First, your whole
Mouth shudders and chokes,
Your tongue revolts.
               Then
The sweetness bursts
And floods.
        Fruit of love,
Bitter, then sweet;
Loss, then restoration.

We eat and we eat.

        *

Flagrante delicto—
Imagine my surprise,
Discovering
That's a Latin
Legal phrase for:
"Apprehended
In the midst of crime."

Immediately, I thought
Of the poor
Cat caught
With its pink tongue
Happily lapping
The bowl of cream
Thoughtlessly
Left on the table.

I may not be a lawyer
But I say:
"Free the kitty!
Release
The innocent pussy!"

So what if I'm only
Pleading
My own case?

Who among us
Could resist
Flagrantly licking
What is so delicious?

                  *

Words crowd around
The beloved:
Fireflies at dusk
Surrounding
A summer oak.

Respectful yet eager,
They sense her
Infinite possibility;
They're drawn
To his heart, large
As a star.
         If they
Aren't summoned
How will they
Come into being?

Some murmur, some
Shout;
      Others
Repeat themselves
Endlessly
In a quiet voice
Like pleading.

        *

Longing alone won't make it so.

But longing *and* words—
Who knows?
         Longing
And a handful of words:

Aren't you halfway to song?

        *

Asking again and again—
What can love do?
Sensing its limits,
Knowing the beloved
Lives in separateness,
Spins around
His or her own mortal center.

Still, the dance compels—
We hear the music
And our feet
Begin to move
And soon our whole body sways.

There must be a reason for this:
We who have never
Sung in our lives
Opening our mouths now.

                    *

The poem no lifeless wonder,
No chunk of amber
With a dead insect inside,
No fossil bearing the delicate
Imprint of a fern.
                    The poem
Made of words: writhing
And alive, making sweet moan.

A thousand years ago, the poet
Felt the beloved's presence,
His eyes filled with tears of joy.

Those same tears in our eyes now.

                    *

Staying afloat by
Zipping across
The surface,
Yet knowing
What I need
Is in the depths.

Moving down
The street so
Fast that all
The faces
Become one blur.

I have to stop
Right now,
Stand
Stock-still
And look at her.

*

Poems that unbutton
And caress—
Those
Are the ones
The young
Sing best.

Yet even
At my age
Still feeling
Eros
At the heart
Of it
Though I'm
Chastened
By time,
Made
Chaste by it.

When my body
Withered
I tried to
Replace it
With wisdom.

When that
Proved vapid
I had to admit
I'd come
Full circle
And needed to start
All over again
As if I'd just
Arrived
In Eden
And was greeted by:

"*A* is for *apple*."

FROM The Book of Reading and Writing,
Which Is the Book of Poets and Poems

There on the page
Poets building
Their word-ships.

Lines they dream
Are shapely
As the beloved's.

Their own form
Of worship.

Riding the wild
River of the world.

*

Space we make
With our arms—
How briefly the beloved
Rests there.

Space the poem makes
In our hearts—
Maybe forever.

*

Reading the poem
Of the beloved
At least twice—
Reading it aloud.

Reading it first
So we can hear
Her plea clearly.

Reading it again
So she can hear ours.

        *

If not for those black scratches
On the page
Where would I be?

Words connecting
The world
To the wound,

Connecting them both to me.

        *

How could that Chinese poet,
Dead two thousand years,
Know how much
We love the world?

If only we could talk
To him as he talks
To us in his poem.
If only we could say
How much his words
Mean to us.
          Quick,
Write it down in the Book.
Send it to him.
Two thousand years from now.

        *

You say you found the poem—
Good for you.
                    Often
For me, it was the other way
Around—
                    I was simply
Skimming, the words
No more
Than a blur on the page,

When the poem reached up
With both hands
To grab my lapels.

What a fervent kiss it gave!

                    *

Moving by hints and piths,
The poem explains
Nothing yet seems
To reveal so much . . .

Half in this world,
Half in some other—
Can the song be trusted?

Who cares, as long
As it does its job:
Brings news of the beloved.

                    *

The poet might wish
To put a ship
In a bottle,
But what about the waves?

In the model, they're
Only blue plaster
Teased into tufts and billows.

You can't bottle
The beloved—
No matter how
Transparent and shapely
The vessel
That contains him,
How clear the glass
In which
She's encased.

Ship in a bottle
On the shelf—quite
A marvel.
        The Book
On the shelf—
Shattering what holds it,
Showering us all
With its salty spray.

        *

Way back then when they
Decided to build
The Tower of Babel
Everyone still spoke
A single language:
That of unregulated passion.

It was the same language God
Taught Eve and Adam,
Who, in turn, passed it
Along to Cain
And Abel, their offspring.

When, millennia later,
We poets struggle
To construct
Our own Tower of Poems,
We gabble and cluck
In a thousand
Different tongues
Yet it all comes
To the same
Thing: the buzz and din of love.

*

Lead of the heart,
Gold of song.

Alchemy of grief
The poem performs.

*

I thought I was hunting
For a poem. Hours spent
Leafing through dusty
Books, huge anthologies.

And all that time, the poem
Was stalking me.
Tiger, burning in the forests

Of the night, eager
To devour my heart.

No, not my whole heart,
Only the rotten parts,
Only what needed
To be renewed.

Only what needed.

*

Suffering, grief, death—
Be foolish not
To admit it:
Themes
In the Book
As heavy as lead.

How then when
We open it
Does it
Rest
So lightly
In our palms?

As if the pages
Were wings
So eager
To fly
They need
To be glued to its spine.

*

That voice,
It's almost
My own.

No, it's
Coming
From a poem.

It means
I'm not alone.

*

How is it those short lines
Zigzag
Down like lightning?

How did Emily
Dickinson
Write those poems?

I bet the beloved
Stood beside her,
Handing her
Words like spears.

What a nightstorm
In the heart!
Each phrase
Bursting
Its ghastly flash,
Followed by sudden dark.

*

Bright scissors
Shining
Blades of song

Free me free me
Once again
From
The invisible
Web
The entangling
Net
I weave myself

Inside
My spider head

*

And all that rage,
Because they
Hurt you
When you were small.

His fist that struck
Your body
Stopped
At the surface,
Bruised the skin.

Yet it also sank
Invisibly in,
Met no resistance
Till it
Reached your heart.

Sing it out proudly—
A song
Of purifying wrath:

That one power
The powerless have.

                *

Rending it, tearing it
Into a thousand pieces.

But still, you're alive.

And love itself didn't end.

How slowly the poem . . .
What a strange way to mend.

                *

Don't bother to ask
For the Book at the library:
It's always checked out.
You'd have to conclude
No one ever returns it.

Better to put together
Your own version:
The poems and songs
You love.
            The ones
That saved you when
You were young

And suffered.
                    And also
Those that consoled you,
When you were older.

                    *

As if that poem
Stared
Straight at you.

As if it had eyes.

Why be surprised?

To see you through,
First
It has to see you.

                    *

Some phrases move
Slow as a worm
Chewing
A tunnel
Through dirt.
Others, swift as a bird.

Always it's the beloved
They're seeking.

She could be hiding
Above;
He could be
Buried below.

Sorrow-songs, trying
Their best
To digest
The thick dark.

Songs of joy—
Whizzing past
So fast they're
Gone before we notice.

*

Scattered randomly
In the Book—
Those poems
We love most.

If we wish to know
The secret
Constellation
That rules our days,

There they are—

Urgent stars
It's up to us to connect.

*

Clutching a bottle of wine,
Petrarch follows his shepherd
Guide. They're trudging up
The steep slopes of Mont
Ventoux.

What he's up to
Is pretty much without
Precedent (at least
In the West):
         Climbing
A mountain
Just for the heck of it.

True, he's also one more
Trapped poet
Of the Middle Ages
Searching for some way out
That doesn't lead to God.

Now he's reached the top
And suddenly *gets* it:

This huge vista his eyes
Are taking in—it
Mirrors the world inside him.

Uncorking the bottle, he
Gazes south, frightened
But brave.
         Biting
His lip hard, he tastes the sea.

*

Praxilla's single poem—
It made her
A fifth-century BC
One-hit wonder.
           It briefly
Topped the charts:

Lament from that bleak
And cheerless Afterworld,
Which was the best
Greeks could imagine,
Even for their greatest heroes.

Those three lines—nothing
But a little list of things
Adonis missed most:

Stars and moon and sun
And the taste of ripe cucumbers.

*

Going to the reading,
Hoping the poet
Will read your poem.

Not the one you wrote
But the one
Written just for you,

That one you've never heard.

*

The poet approaches the lectern—
We've bought another lottery
Ticket, made another investment
In the effort to express human
Passion in a shareable way.

If the poems are bad, the hour
Will seem to go on forever.

If a single poem moves us
Or even a single line
We'll enter eternity briefly
And the gift will shine.

*

The beloved is still.

But also still with us.

All the poems agree,
Even the ones that grieve.

*

The older I get and the more
I write the more I think
About Keats—
How the vowels
He loved plumped
And ripened his lines
Until
They fell away
From his tree of self
So others such as me
Could savor
Those phrases as he once did.

I used to assume they were
Just luscious
Mouth-fruit—
But the more I say them
Aloud the more

I can taste,
Inside each word he loved,
A dense seed,
A something-not-yet-realized—

As if his own death dreamed
A future in which
That word-husk
Split apart
In the dark cave
Of another's mouth
To extend downward
One pleasure-root;
Upward, one stalk of thought.

*

Totally determined
To not let
My guard down.

Allowing no one
Close.
      Permitting
Nothing
That approached
To escape
My ruthless scrutiny.

Armored against grief—
That was me.

And then to be ambushed
By a silly song—

And the beloved
Back again,
As if he'd never gone.

*

Time pummels the whole globe
With catastrophe
And weather—
Why be surprised
It also tests poems?

So what if it's old?
So what if it's been
Wept over for centuries?

Notice—not a single phrase
Is blurred on the page.

Here they are: words
Arranged in hopeful lines,
Patient
As seeds in their furrows.

Say them aloud.

What is your voice if not the rain?

*

Even when the words said
No, the song said,
"Still, you can long."

Even when the world said
"Gone," the poem said,
"Continue to hope."

I stumble and blunder.
All I know is my hunger.

Overflowing with sensations—
Eager to turn them to words
And cover the paper.

Other times, tempted to leave it
Blank—as if to lure her to its still pool.

*

Elegy for Jane Kenyon

1947–1995

Beside me on the plane
An old woman reads
A green pocket Bible,
Its tissue pages
Thin as a fly's wing.
Below, the Monongahela
Winds among smokestacks
And morning fog.

I'm journeying
To your funeral
Having left behind my students
And a final exam
Someone else must present:

Why do you write?
What does poetry mean?
Does it have a purpose
Beyond the personal?

~

Out past my own grief
I hear your lyrics
Shaping pain
Or giving joy the name
Of some common flower:
Daffodil, peony, Queen Anne's lace.

What the self extends: leaf
By leaf, or the whole
Blossom at once—
Pattern we can't explain.

~

Long ago, a teacher told me
About a poetry contest
In Spain.
          Third prize:
A silver rose; second,
A gold.
          The winner
Holding her real rose,
The earth already
Calling its petals home.

*

Young, I took it all so
Personally
When things vanished.

There's a word for that:
Inconsolable.

You'd think, as I
Grew older,
I'd have adjusted
To the simple fact
That everything's
Borne away
On a ceaseless flood.

But then, I'd never have
Become a lyric poet—

Someone with a grudge
Against the world,

Against the world he loves.

        *

Words not just the empty
Shells of things.
Alive, darting
Like minnows in a stream:
Flash and shimmer.

And the water itself:
The flow of our feelings—
Ripple and purl;
The tiny whirlpool

That holds the leaf
In a brief, dizzy embrace
Then lets it go.

*

Sometimes the poem
Changes you slowly
As if eroding the old life.

You have to be patient
With the way it unfolds,
One line at a time.

So unlike the beloved:
All at once and forever.

*

To believe so
Completely
In that
Single poem—

How could you
Do that
If the poem
Didn't also
Believe in you?

*

The critic Hazlitt, on a visit
To the Lake District,
Noticed somber Wordsworth

Paced his closed-in garden
To the regular, iambic meters
He composed in as he strolled;

Noticed also how the wilder
One, Coleridge, when they
Went for walks,
Kept veering off the path
To scramble up steep
Slopes on hands and knees
With urgent, spasmodic
Gestures reminiscent
Of rhythms in his own poems.

The body, the body in motion.

And the beloved—forever
Elusive, always a few feet ahead
Of the poet—just out of reach—

And all that longing turned into song.

*

All the different books you read—
You were searching
For the one Book.

All the poems you read,
And what you really sought
Was the one poem.

And when you found it
Weren't you lifted up?
Didn't you become lighter?

Transparent even, so that
Someone looking at you
Could see the world,
Could see the world inside you?

*

Here's how it is:
Your hair thins even
As your mind declines.

But why do I bother
Warning you
Of what you already
Know:
       It sucks
To be old.
The young are
(Necessarily)
Merciless.
           Oblivion
Doesn't wait
For you—
It's already arrived.

Most of the books
You open:
Nothing but
Coffins that talk.

Lucky for you,
There are a few
Vital and alive—
As if the author

Were there
In your room,
Urgently sharing
What he or she
Felt
And learned

During that brief spell
They lived
On earth.

        *

"The whole country torn
By war. Only mountains
And rivers remain."
So begins Du Fu's poem
Of witness that outlived
The strife it was born from.

On all of us, history imposes
Its grim conditions,
Conditions everyone
Dreads but none
Can predict or control.

What we know: always
The beloved is dying;
Always, rampant violence.

Yet always the soul resists,
And part of this
Is someone somewhere
Writing a poem
And someone else waiting

(Sometimes for centuries)
To read it—someone
Who needs it
So as not to yield to despair.

*

When I was young I wanted
So many things: gadgets
And clothes and cars.

When I was older
I wanted to travel
And eat good food.

Now I want to study
The book of the world:
Every vanishing page.

Now I want to read
The Book of the beloved
Whose every poem
Laughs at the grave.

*

It's what you could call
An exhuming exam:

"You think I'm dead,
But maybe I'm not."

Whitman used to say that
Quite a lot.

After all,
We're still reading his lines.

Alive or dead?
                    Please define.

                    *

Wilfred Owen's hunched
Over his shovel,
Muttering about
Corpse-stench, mustard gas.

And no matter how loud
We shout, he won't look up.

His ears are ruptured;
His brain, concussed
From gigantic artillery
Explosions.
                    He's dug
Enough trenches
To crisscross the entire
Twentieth century
Yet no line is deep enough
To save a single one of us.

                    *

This huge bridge, cabled
Harp strung
Between two cities,
Heart stretched
Taut
Between two shores.

It's here Hart Crane
Paused,
Where others
Had stood
Who couldn't stand
The tension
And chose to leap.

He didn't—he chose to sing.

*

Nothing? Not so much
As a hint or glimpse?

Nowhere in the whole
Book could you
Find it—a poem
That succinctly
Spoke your sorrow?

Seems improbable;
But let's not argue.

And please, don't
Brood or fume
As if you were
Deliberately excluded.

Here's what you must do:

Write it out yourself,
Slip it between two pages.

*

Well, of course
The motive's
Obvious:
He wrote
That poem
To save
A life:
His own.

An odder fact
Much
Harder
To explain:

How it leaped
Huge gaps
Of space
And time

And now
It's saving mine.

                    *

Gerard Manley Hopkins put it succinctly:
The mind has cliffs that are
"Sheer, no-man-fathomed."

He himself had clung to more
Than one. He knew how
Vast and frightening
It can be inside
And never denied
His brain was mostly
A landscape of chasms.

In fact, he descended
Again and again,
Clutching notebook and pen,
To the bottom of the deepest and darkest.

*

As Shakespeare noted: poets
Have a lot in common
With lunatics
And besotted lovers—
Except the poet's eyes
Are free to rove "in a fine
Frenzy rolling," and so
They take in both heaven
And earth (and I'd add
"Hell" as well)—
Take in all three realms,
And also
That wild one inside us.

Not to mention what's going on
In the beloved's head
And heart—that double
Mystery no one's ever
Solved.
      How to untangle
It all and make it plain?

"Grab your pen," that was
The Bard's advice.
         His
One command?
"Write like crazy!
It's your only chance to stay sane."

*

All those poets for
All those
Centuries—
       Each
Pitting his faith
Against fate

Setting her passion
Against
The beloved's
Vanishing

Giving all they had
And leaving
What?
       Sometimes
A whole
Poem
       Often only
An image or
A single phrase
Dense
With longing and praise.

*

A bit of joy, a dollop of longing,
A tear or two for the salt.
A drop of blood for lost
Love, a small bone
To remind us
Of our final home.

These
Are the main ingredients.

Heirloom recipe for
A thousand poems;
Passed along:
                    Parent to child
Then repeated
Down through generations . . .

Feeds us still. Fills us.
Sustains both brain and heart.

                    *

More stores being built
On the corner.
                    More things
To buy and sell.
                    The beloved
Is lost—she can't be
Bought; he can't be sold.

For the price of a poem
The beloved is yours again.

If you can't afford that,
Write one of your own.

                    *

His song was about the world,
She sang of what she saw,
And yet it was always
The beloved's own being

That was the theme
Of that beautiful music.

Sometimes it was words,
Sometimes only the body's
Movements or an expression
Fleeting across the face.

And now the singer himself
Has fled. Now her silence
Is absolute.

Now I open the Book,
Hoping to hear that song again.

*

As I get older and nearer
To my last poem, I often
Ponder Coleridge
And how much he left unfinished.

I think of him as a young man,
Stoned on opium,
Glimpsing that imaginary
Garden for the first time . . .

Even then he was beginning
To suffer the agonies
Of procrastination
That would haunt him
All his days.
                 He believed
In a Christian heaven.
I don't. I prefer *paradise*,

Which is a Persian word
Meaning "walled garden"—
A green and fountained place
In a mostly bleak world
(Which works for me
As one definition of poetry).

I hope he's there, safe
From the hell of this world
Or any other.
               I hope
It's at last completed
And he lives inside it:
That stately pleasure-dome
He and Kubla Khan
Began so many years ago.

FROM The Book of My Own Remembering

Why should it all
Be lost?
Why should time
Take away
That day by the river?

Surely, the storerooms
Of oblivion
Are full to bursting.
Surely, to bring back
That single scene
In all its glory
Wouldn't harm
The order of things.

If only in the words
Of a song or poem.
If only for a moment,
Restoring that moment.

*

I was born on a small farm,
Grew up
Among apple orchards.

I loved exploring
Swamps as a kid.

How does someone
Become a person?

There's a world full of
Things and people.

Feelings and vague notions
Move around inside you.

And words go through
Your head,
Though few of them get said.

*

Childhood swimming hole,
The bridge across it.
I held on so long,
Dangled there, afraid.
Hoping somehow
I could gauge
The water's depth
Before I let go.

No shame in that:
Any sane person
Might have felt fear.

But I was wrong: it
Wasn't shallow or shatter.
It was deep,
Deeper than I could imagine.

*

I sat at my kindergarten desk
Surrounded by others,
Either cheerful
Or bored, who were
Cutting
The requisite circles

With ease
Or slicing down
Straight, penciled lines
As the teacher directed.

I did my dutiful
Left-handed best,
But the scissors
Hurt my fingers
In a minor,
Distracting way
And I was too young
To realize the handle
Was biased
For a right-hand child,
So all I could do
Was cut in clumsy zigzags
And feel like a fool.

Staring hard at the blades,
I tried to *will* them
To obey,
Who couldn't conceive
I was being freed
That day
By those little silver wings
Of a bird
Intent on the erratic,
Authentic pattern
Of its *own* flight
Through a sky of colored paper.

*

When I was just a kid
I wanted to be a painter.

Even then I thought
If I could stop time

Every moment
Would be perfect:

The horses bowed
Over the water trough,

The chickens
Clustered by their shed,

The lonely boy
Skating on the frozen stream.

*

Half-dead cherry tree
Across the road
From my childhood house,
We climbed you
For the few bunches
Of fruit you produced.

Often, beneath our feet,
Branches snapped,
Exposing the soft
White rot.
        You had
Become a part
Of the fenceline:
Amber resin oozed
From your bark

Where wire was stapled.
You closed on each strand
Like a horse clamping
On a bit—puckered scar
Where you took it in
Toward your slow heart.

*

On the lawn, beside the red house,
My mother taught me
To slice deep circles around
The dandelions
With the sharp point
Of my trowel
So when I pulled them
The taproots came up, too.

She wore a blue dungaree jacket,
Her braided hair
Tied up in a paisley bandanna.

We knelt there, mother and son,
Digging in silence
In the dusk of late summer.

*

Little card inked with your
Disdain—O Mrs. Malone,
To you I was nothing
But "head in the clouds"
Or "always
With his nose in a book."

Not to mention that D–
For "plays well with others."

To think—only third grade
And (proud prophet)
Already you had my number.

*

All morning, with gloved hands,
My brothers and I
Grip and tug burdock
And the tough, fibrous stalks
Of chicory. We knock roots
Against boot soles to jar
The clumped earth loose.

When the brush pile's tangled
Mound is high enough,
We set it ablaze and stand
Squinting into the heat,
Waiting for the branch
That always rises whole
And flaming, ready
To sprint to where it settles
And put out its sparks
With quick, flat
Slaps of our bamboo rakes.

At dusk, easing down
On porch steps to unlace
My boots, I pause—
Smoke, sweat, dirt, and flesh
Makes this smell I love—
I cup my face in my hands
And breathe deeply.

*

It's Memorial Day. After our march
From the Hudson to the top of Cemetery Hill
We Boy Scouts proudly endure
The sermons and hot sun while Girl Scouts
Loll among graves in the maple shade.
When members of the veteran's honor guard
Aim their bone-white rifles skyward and fire
I glimpse, beneath one metal helmet,
The salmon-pink flesh of Mr. Webber's nose,
Restored after shrapnel tore it.

~

Friends who sat near me in school died in Asia,
Now lie here under new stones that small flags flap
Beside.
            It's fifth-grade recess: war stories.
Mr. Webber stands before us and plucks
His glass eye from its socket, holds it high
Between finger and thumb. The girls giggle
And scream; the awed boys gape.
The fancy pocket watch he looted
From a shop in Germany ticks on its chain.

*

I remember him falling beside me,
The dark stain already seeping across his parka hood.
I remember screaming and running the half mile to our house.
I remember hiding in my room.
I remember that it was hard to breathe
And that I kept the door shut in terror that someone would enter.
I remember pressing my knuckles into my eyes.

I remember looking out the window
To where an ambulance had backed up
Over the lawn to the front door.
I remember someone hung from a tree near the barn
The deer we'd killed just before I shot my brother.
I remember toward evening someone came with soup.
I slurped it down, unable to look up.
In the bowl, among the vegetable chunks,
Pale shapes of the alphabet bobbed at random
Or lay in the shallow spoon.

*

The field where my brother died—
I've walked there since.
Weeds and grasses, some chicory
Stalks; no trace of the scene
I still can see: a father
And his sons bent above
A deer they'd shot,
Then screams and shouts.

Always I arrive too late
To take the rifle
From the boy I was,
Too late to warn him
Of what he can't imagine:
How quickly people vanish;
How one moment you're standing
Shoulder to shoulder,
The next you're alone in a field.

*

"He's already in heaven," she said,
"Sitting down to feast with Jesus."
Back then, if I had been eight or ten
And she had been a peer instead
Of an adult, I might have said:
"You must have a hole in your head,"
Meaning: you must be crazy.

But I was twelve and though
I thought she was insane I was too
Polite and frightened to say as much.
And the hole was not a metaphor
But one a bullet had made that day
In my brother's head. And I
Was the one who put it there.

I wonder if she had been thinking
Of the painted window
In our dinky church: the one
Where Jesus sat at a picnic table
With bread and a jug of something?
Was it an image of the wedding
At Cana? Or the Last Supper
Before any of the other guests
Had arrived?
                    He didn't look
Lonely, He just sat with His arms
Spread and His empty hands open
As if He were patiently waiting
For someone to put something in them:
A plate of food? Some nails? A gun?

Who knows what He was up to,
What He thought or felt?

He was in His world
And I was in mine.
This is all I knew that was true:
I was alive; my brother was dead.
When I closed my eyes I saw him
Lying at my feet.
                        I knew
God and I were through,
And after that what is there?

I imagined I was floating
Alone in a vast abyss
Like a little cloud,
But I wasn't—I was falling
As fast as a material body can,
But the distance was infinite
And there was nothing near
By which to judge
What was happening and so
It seemed I wasn't moving at all.

                    *

If I wrote in a short story
Or novel that when my father
Was young, about thirteen,
He and his best friend
Stole a rifle from the car trunk
Of a man who worked
For his family, then took
Paper plates from the kitchen
And went out to a field,
Intending to toss them
Into the air and shoot them . . .

That there'd been an accident
And he killed his best friend.

Sad, but believable—it happens
More often than you'd imagine
In the country.
                                    But then I add:
My dad grew up, married,
Had four sons, gave
The two oldest a
Shotgun each when they were
Twelve and ten,
So they could all hunt pheasants.
And when I turned twelve,
He gave me a rifle—a .22.
And that same year
We went hunting deer
In a far field on our property
And my gun, which I didn't know
Was loaded, went off
And killed my younger brother
Who was standing beside me.
Two boys, my father and I,
Barely in their teens,
Killing accidentally two others
They loved—that kind
Of coincidence isn't credible
In fiction, much less in a poem
Where you're not allowed
To describe too much
Or explain, or ascribe motives,
Because each word is precious
And the fewer you use
The better the poem.

And yet,
I'm telling you it's true,
It really happened.
                    All of us
Can see the pattern here—
Two young boys kill
Someone they love
By accident.
                    But do you
Think God planned it?
And if so, why?
Do you think my father
Unconsciously arranged
A repetition, hoping
It would end differently?

I'm happy for you if you
Can explain it
To your satisfaction.
I can't.
                    I'm only telling you
About it because
It's factual; it happened.
And because I want you to know
How strange life is.

                    *

For me, my brother
Was the first beloved,
The first departure
That tore my heart.
I was so stricken
When he died
I couldn't speak.

I was young
And knew nothing
About the Book.

It was years before
I learned poems
Could be letters
The living address
To their dead.
Years before I knew
Poems in the Book
Were answers they send.

*

My mother so soon to die,
And me really
Still a child.

How driving at night,
She used to sing
Old songs.
                My favorite
Was "Down in the Valley"—
Melancholy tune
Whose refrain went:
"Angels in heaven
Know I love you."

Sitting close beside her,
I misheard
That line, as if
It paused in the middle
While the singer
Considered

A celestial offer
And then declined:

As if it meant:
"Angels in heaven?
No, I love *you.*"

Such a choice
Impressed me,
And even then made sense.

*

At the Sunday-school picnic
I watch a fisherman haul
Waterweeds and a ragged
Hat from the lake.
A whisper among
The charcoal smoke:
"You shall not live forever."

Under bare feet, warmth
Of pine needles as she
And I climb in bathing suits
Up a path to the tower;
Icy damp of its stairs.

We never touch. We'll
Never meet again,
But as we lean together
On the balcony,
I glimpse eternity
Beneath her pale, green suit:
Small breasts, pink nipples.

*

From the houses of American engineers,
Laughter and the sound of ice
In glasses.
         The pastor sets out benches
On the tennis court; it's time to sing
Hymns in Creole: "Rock of Ages"
In this land where soft stone crumbles.

Mennonite nurses move through twilight
Toward their bungalows.
                Sweet reek
Of jasmine; stench of mango rinds
And urine in the cactus hedge.
Red ants gather in a lizard's eye.

          (Deschapelles, Haiti, 1961)

*

I pass the old beggar who sits,
Sucking on a corncob pipe, in the shade
Of a huge gray mapou tree,
Its roots stuck with candle stubs,
Gifts for the ghosts inside;

Down the hill past the stench
Of the courtyard where burros are tethered,
Across the parched lawn where kin
Of the sick squat beside charcoal
Fires cooking rice and red beans;

Up the steps and through a double set
Of screen doors that never yet kept
Malaria out. Mother, I'm coming
Down the halls toward the room
Where you lie, coughing and soon to die.

And if I had known, as no one did,
That this would be the last visit,
What could I have brought? All I have:
The sweat and sights and smells
Of Haiti, under my small straw hat.

(Hôpital Albert Schweitzer, Deschapelles, Haiti, 1961)

         *

It was a tiny, nameless, emerald bird
I glimpsed only once
Flitting across a path I walked
When I was a kid living
In Haiti shortly before
My mother died
And was buried there
Under a stone
Beneath a dusty tree.

Whenever I hear "Green
Sleeves," my mother's
Favorite song,
I think of her and see that bird.
Sometimes the heart's so full
It's a wonder it doesn't burst asunder.

         *

My entire youth I hid
My shame
In a secret place
Of which I was
Perversely proud:
A heart inside my heart.

Then a high school teacher
Showed me a poem,
Encouraged me
To write my own,
And suddenly
It all became obvious:

To suffer in silence
Was self-violence.

To speak my grief,
Relief.

And to sing:
That was the great thing.

*

"It happened for me at sixteen"
Should be the opening line
To a hymn of praise
For all the joy I felt
Squirming in the backseat
With a girl,
          But actually
Refers to the first serious
Poem I wrote
And how it changed my life.

Wordsworth put it this way:
"I made no vows, but vows
Were then made for me."

Poetry works like that:
It steals your adolescent
Soul and binds it
In a joyful hell of rhythms
You can hear but can't
Quite replicate in words.

From that moment on
You're its funky monk.

Good luck, you'll need it.

Soon you'll have squandered
Most of your days trying
To say it right.
                    Bad news is:
It can't be done.

Good news is: the struggle's fun.

                    *

If there's a god of amphetamine he's also the god of wrecked lives, and it's only he who can explain how my doctor father, with the gift of healing strangers and patients alike, left so many intimate dead in his wake.

If there's a god of amphetamine, he's also the god of recklessness, and I ask him to answer.

He's the god of thrills, the god of boys riding bikes down steep hills with their hands over their heads.

He's the god of holy and unholy chance: the god of soldiers crossing a field and to the right of you a man falls dead and to the left also and you are still standing.

If there's a god of amphetamine, he's the god of diet pills, who is the god of the '50s housewife who vacuums all day and whose bathroom is spotless and now it is evening as she sits alone in the kitchen, polishing her chains.

He's the god of the rampant mind and the god of my father's long monologues by moonlight in the dark car driving over the dusty roads.

He's the god of tiny, manic orderings in the midst of chaos, the god of elaborate charts where Greg will do this chore on Monday and a different one on Tuesday and all the brothers are there on the chart and all the chores and all the days of the week in a minuscule script no one can read.

If there's a god of amphetamine, my father was his hopped-up acolyte who leaped out of bed one afternoon to chase a mouse through the house, shouting, firing his .38 repeatedly at the tiny beast scurrying along the wall while Jon wailed for help from the next room.

If there's a god of amphetamine, he's the god of subtle carnage and dubious gift who lives in each small pill that tastes of electricity and dust.

If there's a god of amphetamine, my father was its high priest, praising it, preaching its gospel, lifting it like a host and intoning: "Here in my hand is the mystery: a god alive inside a tiny tablet. He is a high god, a god of highs—he eats the heart to juice the brain and mocks the havoc he makes, laughing at all who stumble. Put out your tongue and receive it."

All afternoon they bobbed above us—
Three giant charcoal portraits
Of Goodman, Schwerner, and Chaney,
Civil rights martyrs whose tortured
Bodies had just been discovered
In the red clay wall
Of a dam in rural Mississippi.

Staring up at their flat, larger-
Than-life faces, I envied
The way they gazed at the gray
Ocean and the gray buildings
With the calm indifference
Of those whose agonies were over.
Myself, I was a frightened teenager
At my first demonstration,
Carrying a placard that demanded
The seating of a mixed delegation
From a Southern state.
                              No one
Prepared me for the crowd's
Hostility, the names we were called.

Still, we chanted the slogan reason
Proposed: "One man, one vote."
And still it held—the small shape
We made on the dilapidated boardwalk—
Reminding me now of magic circles
Medieval conjurers drew
To protect themselves from demons
Their spells had summoned up.

(Democratic National Convention, Atlantic City, 1964)

*

On a Highway East of Selma, Alabama

July 1965

As the sheriff remarked: I had no business being there. He was right, but for the wrong reasons. Among that odd crew of volunteers from the North, I was by far the most inept and least effective. I couldn't have inspired or assisted a woodchuck to vote.

In fact, when the sheriff's buddies nabbed me on the highway east of Selma, I'd just been released from ten days of jail in Mississippi. I was fed up and terrified; I was actually fleeing north and glad to go.

~

In Jackson, they'd been ready for the demonstration. After the peaceful arrests, after the news cameras recorded us being quietly ushered onto trucks, the doors were closed and we headed for the county fairgrounds.

Once we passed its gates, it was a different story: the truck doors opened on a crowd of state troopers waiting to greet us with their nightsticks out. Smiles beneath mirrored sunglasses and blue riot helmets; smiles above badges taped so numbers didn't show.

For the next twenty minutes, they clubbed us, and it kept up at intervals, more or less at random, all that afternoon and into the evening.

Next morning we woke to new guards who did not need to conceal their names or faces. A little later, the FBI arrived to ask if anyone had specific complaints about how they'd been treated and by whom.

But late that first night, as we sat bolt upright in rows on the concrete floor of the cattle barn waiting for mattresses to arrive, one last precise event: a guard stopped in front of the ten-year-old Black kid next to me. He pulled a FREEDOM NOW pin from the kid's shirt, made him put it in his mouth, then ordered him to swallow.

~

That stakeout at dusk on Route 80 east of Selma was intended for someone else, some imaginary organizer rumored to be headed toward their dismal, godforsaken town. Why did they stop me?

The New York plates, perhaps, and that little bit of stupidity: the straw hat I wore, a souvenir of Mississippi.

Siren-wail from an unmarked car behind me—why should I think they were cops? I hesitated, then pulled to the shoulder. The two who jumped out waved pistols, but wore no uniforms or badges. By then, my doors were locked, my windows rolled. Absurd sound of a pistol barrel rapping the glass three inches from my face: "Get out, you son of a bitch, or we'll blow your head off."

When they found pamphlets on the backseat they were sure they'd got the right guy. The fat one started poking my stomach with his gun, saying, "Boy, we're gonna dump you in the swamp."

~

It was a long ride through the dark, a ride full of believable threats, before they arrived at that hamlet with its cinder-block jail.

He was very glad to see it, that adolescent I was twenty years ago. For eight days he cowered, stinking of dirt and fear, in his solitary cell. He's cowering there still, waiting for me to come back and release him by turning his terror into art. But consciously or not, he made his choice and he's caught in history.

And if I reach back now, it's only to hug him and tell him to be brave, to remember that Black kid who sat beside him in the Mississippi darkness. And to remember that silence shared by guards and prisoners alike as they watched in disbelief the darkness deepening around the small shape in his mouth, the taste of metal, the feel of the pin against his tongue.

It's too dark for it to matter what's printed on the pin; it's too dark for anything but the brute fact that someone wants him to choke to death on its hard shape.

And still he refuses to swallow.

*

When I was eighteen and a volunteer
In the Movement,
I was kidnapped at gunpoint
In rural Alabama
And imprisoned in a murderous town.

Inexplicably, after the first beatings
And the believable threats,
After they'd locked me
In a solitary cell,
They let me keep a book of Keats.

I was sick and scared.
It seemed probable I would die there
As others like me had and would.

That's when his nightingale ode
First made sense—
How he rose above his woes
On imagination's wings,
Though for me it was more
Of a ladder:
Rungs and lifts of escape.

Reading deep into the night,
I'd climb with each line
Until I was high in a treetop
With that bird I could just
Glimpse by shinnying up
The bars of my cell:
                                    Mockingbird
In the magnolia, across the moonlit road.

(Hayneville, Alabama, July 1965)

*

How small the eyes of hate.
I'm not making this up
Or being metaphorical.
A man held a gun against
My head and I saw how
Small his eyes were
With what they refused
To take in of the world.
This happened beside

A small highway
In Alabama in 1965.
What history called
The Civil Rights
Movement;
What I call:
The tiny eyes of hate.

*

How large the eyes of love.
How the pupils dilate
With desire (I'm not
Making this up: science
Has proved it's true).

Those eyes wide
And glistening: gates
Thrown open. What's
Inside free to flow
Out as feeling,
And the whole world
And the beloved
Welcome to enter.

*

Young, we waved flags
That were scarlet or black—
Pure hues that thrilled us.

We dreamed of sacrificing
Everything
In a single extravagant gesture,
Because all we had

Was ourselves
And we felt like nothing.

We had not met the beloved yet.

*

Like any other man,
I was born with a knife
In one hand
And a wound in the other.

In the house
Where I was raised
All the mirrors
Were painted black.

So many years
Before the soft key
Of the beloved's tongue
Unlocked my body.

*

For years I couldn't speak
My grief—
Sensed I needed to wait
For my
Wounds to close.

Then I feared it was too
Late, feared my sorrow
Had become so
Deep-rooted,

Wrapped so tight
Around the beloved's bones

That nothing could be spoken.

*

When I lived alone in New York, studying
To become a poet, the city ran a campaign against
Kids leaving school.
                    Posters in the subway read:
"Yesterday I couldn't even spell 'drop-out'—
Now I are one."
                    Vivid but mean, it burned
Into my memory—I who felt lost and unmoored
In my own culture, who yearned
To turn all that was in me into words.

As if language came easily to anyone;
As if grammar didn't mock us all;
As if the anguish and mystery
Of being a person were supposed to fit in a system.

*

We'd only just met, were
Driving in your car
When the axle broke
In a small town. No hotel,
No money. We had
To sleep in a field.
It was dark when we lay
Down. Cold, though
It was summer. Trying

To stay warm with all
Our clothes on. For a while
I was the blanket and you
The body, then the other
Way around: one on top
And then the other. And
In the middle of the night
We argued because you took
Your boots off. I thought
You would be colder;
You knew: the boots too
Tight, the circulation
Cut off, better bare feet
Than that. And a skunk
Wandered by in the dark;
So close we could hear it
As well as smell it.
And at dawn we found
We'd slept by a pond,
And a kingfisher paused
On a branch above it.
Its iridescent feathers.
And on a hill across
The small valley, the name
Of the town spelled
In white rocks: "Castle
Creek." This story is true
And happened forty years
Ago. And did we know then
We'd be together still?
Which is the beloved,
Which is the world.

for Trisha

*

Our first, exploratory meeting—
Full of mutual suspicions.

How could they be
Overcome?
            In the beginning,
It wasn't even certain
We spoke the same tongue.

At best, they were wildly
Divergent dialects.

A dictionary?
                Years
In the making.
                Key terms?
Still in dispute to this day.

*

If we were two ships
We could have passed
In the ocean and not
Known.
            If we were
Two birds we might
Have been flying
To opposite sides
Of the sky.
            But
We were two bodies
Who bumped
Into each other

And clung.
          Two
Bodies that collided,
Then steadied each other,
Then stayed.

                    *

From the outset,
It was hard for
Us
To see eye to eye.

For my part, I was
Distracted
By the rest of you.

                    *

I like to think "I" and "you"
Came together
As the country of Us
Because
They were destined
For mutual rescue.

Not unlike the word
And the world:

Those entities so eager
To be introduced
So they can fuse
In a way that's
Erotic,
Though not necessarily lewd.

*

Beloved, with your hair
Like a cloud
That half-hides the moon.
With eyes like pools
That disprove stars and depths
In the same sentence.
With fingers as delicate and precise
As brushes Angelico used
To make the Madonna smile.
With occult hands. With
Shoulders like banks of snow
The wind has sculpted.
With breasts that made Krishna
Restless all night, so nothing
Could silence his lonely flute.
With belly of wheat and sable.
With hips like the wave's swell.
With hips that are cliffs
And whose sex is the salty harbor
Of the mariner's dream,
Where he's safe at last from the sea.

for Trisha

*

Back then I thought flowing
Was a flaw in the world;
I didn't know
It was simply its main
Way of being.

I thought going *always*
Meant grief,
Meant something
Was wrong
And someone I loved
I couldn't hold
No matter how strong.

I thought wounding
Only meant losing,
Meant nothing
But loss.

How could I know
It was also another mouth,

Another source of song?

*

Yesterday, against admonishment,
My daughter balanced on the couch back,
Fell, and cut her mouth.

Because I saw it happen, I knew
She was not hurt, and yet
A child's blood's so red
It stops a father's heart.

My daughter cried her tears;
I held some ice
Against her lip.
That was the end of it.

Round and round; bow and kiss.
I try to teach her caution,
She tries to teach me risk.

*

It consists of cliffs and plateaus—
The lyric life I chose.

In the worse phase, I know
Each desperate word
Is only a handhold
And there's a sheer fall below.

In the other, the pressure's
Suddenly gone
And I stroll along
As calm phrases unfold;

Soon, I've become deluded—
My guard's down,
And I'm convinced
It will always be like this:
A steady catalogue
Of my hard-earned bliss.

That's when it opens
Beneath my feet—recurrent abyss.

*

Truth of it is: I was born
With an empty center.

When I find myself there
It's often despair,
But now and then it's Zen.

A leap of faith from a cliff?
I prefer hope
And bring my own rope.

A focused love is a doubled
Devotion—each shrine
I build deepens my mind.

Only when I yearn, do I learn.

And what helps me grow is holy.

*

My mother's joy
Never lasted long.
Her sorrow either.

She walked her path
Into oblivion
Long before I wrote
My first poem.

I see her now,
Resurrected
In my thoughts:

One more beloved
Lighting my way
Into the dark,

One more beloved
Bringing back
From the abyss
Explicable gifts.

*

Meander—it's the name of a river
In Turkey,

Which was called Asia Minor
Way back when.
                    The river
Snaked its slow way
Across a flat valley,
Seemingly in no hurry
To reach the sea.

Which reminds me now
How lucky we were
To see it from the hills
Overlooking that valley,
The two of us standing
In the ruins of a small Greek
Temple in a grove
Redolent of sun-warmed
Pine needles (is there
Anywhere in this world
A smell more intoxicating?).

It wasn't a river anymore—
Hardly even a stream.
Things diminish.
                    We were
Young then and now
We're not.
                    These words
Wander down this page:
Meandering
Like that river now a stream,
Or what was once
A memory and now seems a dream.

                    *

Song of Old Lovers

Our bodies: lock
And key. A drop
Of oil if it's rusty.
Something turns in me.

Our bodies: the sea
And the shore.
The bee
And the flower.
Eternity
Dissolving into hours.

Time is the dial
Sweeping the face;
Time is the turtle
Winning the race.

                    *

All this winter afternoon spent
Reading about ancient
Greek lyric and the invention
Of the simple alphabet—
How those small marks
On papyrus changed
Everything, persuaded
Lyric poets they could
Become immortal.
                    "Someone
Will remember us,"
Wrote Sappho, naming
Herself and those she loved

In poems that are only
Fragments now
And a single one that's whole:
A prayer to Aphrodite.

An old man with a full
Bladder, I pause
To step out back
Where yesterday's flurries
Have made the lawn
A blank page
Into a small corner of which
I piss out the hot stream
Of my own being,
Grateful to be part of that
Holy and hopeless story
By which poets send past death
Their praise of life
And write
Their names on the vanishing page.

PART FOUR

FROM The Book of Words, Which Is the
Book of Listening and Speaking

At my age, you don't
Have to drink
Half a dictionary
To get drunk on words—
Just a sip
Can make you tipsy.

Next, slips of the tongue.
Now you're having fun.

"God so loved the word
He gave his only
Begotten world
That it might be
Redeemed."

Is that what the preacher
Used to say
In my church
When I was a kid?

Maybe I got it wrong—
Truth is, back then,
I wasn't really listening.

*

"And the word
Was made
Fresh"—

Each one
Baked daily.

It's the bread
By which I live.

*

Taking the empty air
Deep in our lungs,
Warming it there,

Extracting from it
What our blood needs,

Then breathing it back
Out as sound
We've added meaning to.

Can anyone show me
A greater miracle
In this—our only world?

*

Not fleeing our agony,
Actually willing to fly
To the heart of it—
If only we let them.

Eager to articulate
Our darkest thoughts
Without despairing.

Or cling to our secrets
And give them shape.

What words will do
If only we'll stop
Trying to make them
Say something
Beautiful that isn't true.

Who among us can speak
Of someone else's
Suffering?

To understand that
We have to listen.

Turning to the Book
To hear
What others felt and feel.

Where did the beloved go?
I've looked in all the poems,
Looked high and low.

Coming toward me,
Blank page in one hand,
Pen in the other.

Coming toward me,
A song on her lips.
Only needing me,
Only needing me for the words.

Vowels woven
Through our songs
As the beloved
Through our life—

Low, lubricious
Moan of *o*
Followed by
The *ah*
Of release

High *e* of grief

And *u*—who
Could forget you?

I could never,
Y would I even try?

                    *

Poets writing words as
Fast as they can,
Trying
To keep up
With the beloved.

No use, really.
Each one—
Only her
For just so long.

By the time
You say it,
He's already gone.

                    *

River inside the river.
World within the world.

All we have is words

To reveal the rose
The rose obscures.

*

Saying the word
Is seizing the world.

Not by the scruff,
Not roughly,
But still fervent,
Still the fierce hug of love.

*

Yes, our human
Time is finite;
That much is obvious.

But I can hear
The infinite knocking
At the door
Of almost every word.

And when they open,
Each of them opens
Into a world.

*

Dull gray bundle of feathers
Pausing
On the dogwood branch—
I doubt it will be there long.

If, during its brief dawdle,
I decide to call it
By its proper name
Could it become a beloved?

Mockingbird poised now
On the pink twig of my tongue.

*

How badly the world needs words.
Don't be fooled
By how green it is,
How it seems to be thriving.

Willow rescues that tree
From its radiant perishing.

How much more so, then,
When you name the beloved.

*

What did someone cynically
Say once: open a vein
And let it flow onto the page?

If only one could
And have words result.

Not seeking self-display,
Seeking release.

Seeking the other
Who is lost inside you.

Seeking to say it out:
Your grief and longing
Bringing the resurrection about.

*

Words, am I
Wrong
To worship you,

To imagine
You are somehow
Exempt
From
The world's flaws?

That *leaf* is
Complete,
Unscarred
By insect
Or wind-tossed twig

And yet also
An essence
That implicates
The world

As a wound
Implies a body?

*

Snow on the tree branch.
Vanished by noon.

That feeling I had—
It's gone, too.

Something about
The wonder of it.

Poem of the snow
On the tree branch.

It's still there.

*

Each thing in the world
Waits for its word—

Hoping we'll name it.

Each object dreams
Of becoming the beloved—

One song could save it.

*

Nouns doing
Their best
To be exact—
Nailing
Themselves
To objects,
Sticking to facts:

This is *this,*
And *that* is *that.*

Then along
Comes
The beloved
Whose
Lightest touch
Bursts all bubbles.

        *

Why try to seize what flows?
Why try to confine,
To clench
In the fist of a poem?

Yet words bring the world
Close
And hold it
If only
For a moment.
                 "Rose
Rose!"
       And doesn't
The tongue love it
Just as much as the nose?

        *

Often just a few notes—
A phrase or refrain

Rising
Above the hubbub—

Needing to lean in
Close to hear it.

Needing to listen
Not

With ears only
But also with my whole life.

*

I don't remember
The first word
I heard.

I won't remember
The last.

How important
They are:
The ones I hear now.

*

If I wanted words, I could
Turn on the TV or radio.
If I wanted the world
I could look out the window.

I want the beloved, who is lost.

Turning to the Book, turning
To words about the world,

Yet wanting neither words
Nor world.
                  Or wanting both,
But more also:
Wanting what I lack,
Wanting my passion back.

                  *

The old philosopher, dying,
Writes a last brief essay
In which he confesses
He wishes he'd learned
More poems by heart.

"The old chestnuts,"
He calls them,
By which he means
The rhyming ones
He loved when young.

"I would have been more
Fully human," he writes.

Reciting, in his last days,
Those he remembers,
As if the Book
Were in his mind
And he reading them aloud,

*Which is the resurrection
Of the body of the beloved,
Which is the world.*

                  *

If you're unsure what words can do,

Imagine being Helen Keller
Who was blind, deaf, dumb
Almost from birth.
Her entire, silent childhood
She was terrified and furious.

By seven, all she'd learned
Was the alphabet
Signed out in her hand
But no idea those gestures
Connected in any way
To the world.
                      And then,
One June afternoon
As another of her agonized
Tantrums subsided, she stood
At the backyard pump
And her teacher began
To spell out, again
And again, with fingertips
On her open palm:
w-a-t-e-r w-a-t-e-r

While over the other: a cool flowing.

                  *

What connects us to the world?
What holds us in it?

You'd think: whatever you love.
Certainly that makes sense;
Certainly we know that's true.

But for poets, it's also words.
If you don't believe me,
Listen to Whitman who
According to his own
Testimony loved everyone
And everything.
        And yet
He felt like an isolated spider
Letting loose its threads
In a windy field—"filaments"
He called them—hoping
They'd catch hold of some
Object and become
"Ductile anchors"
That secured him to this world:

"Filament, filament, filament"—
And what he meant was words.

      *

This or that individual story:
How its details break your heart.
How did she survive
Such agony?
        Is it possible
That that happened
And yet he's still alive?

No. He did die, but he's also
Alive. She moves among
The living, but
Because of this she's also dead.

Yet the beloved can live again,
Needs to—what words are for,
What ears also:
                    To hear this,
To not turn away, to not
Abandon the beloved,
Who has come to us to be saved.

*

"Doggie, doggie!"
The child cries
With glee,
Pointing at the cat
Which has just
Entered the room.

Sometimes, accuracy
Doesn't matter.

Irresistible flow of it
Toward some thing—
Love will not
Be stopped
Or quibbled with.

*

How much love can it hold?
How much of the world
Can it celebrate in words?

We won't know until
The beloved stops singing,
Who's only begun her song.

*

The world spins.
The words whirl.

If I'm not careful
I'll succumb
To a cosmic
Dizziness,
Inside and out.

No wonder
I stick
To short poems,
Little words.

*

Outside our bodies, things
Wait to be named,
To be saved.

And don't they deserve it?
So much hidden inside
Each one,
Such a longing
To become the beloved.

Meanwhile, the sounds
Crowd our mouths,
Press up against
Our lips,
Which
Are such
A narrow exit
For a joy so desperate.

Words, of course, but
Also the silence
Between them.

Like the silence
Between
The beloved and you.
Silence full
Of the unspoken
As a seed is full
Of all
It will become.

No poem made only
Of silence.
No poem
Made only of words.

*

Silence. Does silence
Make things vanish?
Or confirm
Their disappearance?
Is the beloved
Who has died
Buried more deeply
By silence
Than by earth?

Even closed
And locked away

The Book whispers
About the beloved
In dreams.
            Still,
It's a whispering
Difficult to understand,
Impossible almost.

But if we find
The Book and open it,
If we find the poem
That is trying to find us,
The poem the beloved
Wrote and sent out
On the long journey
Toward our heart—if
We find that poem,
It all makes sense
And the silence recedes
Before the beloved's
Quiet voice speaking to us.

                *

I put the beloved
In a wooden coffin.
The fire ate his body;
The flames devoured her.

I put the beloved
In a poem or song.
Tucked it between
Two pages of the Book.

How bright the flames.
All of me burning,
All of me on fire
And still whole.

*

Salt on the roads melts
The ice.
      Salt on the heart
Hardens it.
        That's not
How the Book
Preserves the body.

The bitten tongue
Tastes blood.
      The tongue
Uttering, utters love.

*

When my gaze strays
From the page
I see my mottled hand
Resting on the tabletop,
A tired thing sleeping.

When I read the poem
Aloud, my hand revives.
It wants to dance
In air in time
To the words.
      It wants

To make a sweeping gesture
As if clearing cobwebs
Or yanking back
A heavy curtain
To reveal the world.

                    *

All I remember is the chorus:
"Whatever's begotten
Must rot."
                    Somber tune
That pulsed
From my mother's heart
To impress itself
On my embryo-bones
Where I curled in the dark:

Throb of presence
Followed by the lull of loss.

How I danced even then
To that tune
And never asked
Whether it was sad or happy
Because I knew it was true.

                    *

Balanced on the edge
Of speech,
But the slope is so steep.

To speak is to leap.

Wanting to, but afraid.
Instead, merely
Gazing at the beloved
From the high cliff of love.

*

Time to shut up.
Voltaire said the secret
Of being boring
Is to say everything.

And yet I held
Back about love
All those years:
Talking about death
Insistently, even
As I was alive;
Talking about loss
As if all were loss,
As if the world
Did not return
Each morning.
As if the beloved
Didn't long for us.

No wonder I go on
So. I go on so
Because of the wonder.

*

Some days it's all a blur.
I can't locate the world,

Can't find the beloved.
Can't even find the words.

Maybe I need to lie back
And listen. Maybe
Something's being said
That I haven't yet heard.

Time to stop talking
And let the beloved speak.

Time to trust it all:
To stop searching
And let the beloved seek.

       *

Blossoms scattered in the street
As if the beloved's necklace
Broke.
       Wild night!
No time to stop
And gather each bead.

Let the Book burst asunder—
Let it be nothing but songs of love.

       *

I always supposed
It was words
I was after—
Those
Shining fish
The poem's net gets.

But who knows?
Maybe it was
The sea
Itself
I was trying
To haul on deck.

*

Words, how I loved you
Then—when I
Was young
And you led me
Out of the dark!

How I love you now
Even more,
As the dark approaches.

Knowing life grinds us
And dust
Is what we'll become.

Sensing, likewise,
That the moral
Of our story
Has to do
With being mortal.

Yet love grounds us.

And the beloved
Grows in us:
We are her slow cocoon.

And the poem is a door;
The song, a little window.

*

Intimacy not yet
A science:

No one knows
How or why
Bodies come close
Then recede.

One day, the abyss
Between you
Is infinite
And distance
Mocks your shout.

The next, a whisper's loud.

Who was born so shy
He feared the sound
Of his own voice,
But in time fell in love
With the mellifluous
Flow of words in poems.

Who grew enough
To want to write
His own, and, finally,
To speak them aloud.

Who was afraid to say "I"
Because he knew
It implied
A deep longing for "you."

Fate not just a pair of scissors
Waiting at the end to cut the thread
But there at the beginning,
Spinning the same thread out:
That bright filament of song
Whitman said connects us all—

Spinning out that string of words
With which we wed the world,
With which we espouse the beloved.

Spinning out the poem of our vow.

Between—that's where
Love is.
                    That's why
The beloved needs us
As much
As we need her or him.

                    *

Some of us lucky
Enough to live
In couples,
Yet still we're alone.

Not even the beloved
Can alter
Our bodily solitude.

But she gives it focus;
He gives it hope.

                    *

The world so huge and dark
It swallows our cry.

But we're no longer lost:
The beloved has heard us
And even now approaches.

We move toward each other
Like two words
That will join in a poem.

A small poem, a little song,
But one in which we're not alone.

*

Hold on! Let go!

A classic tale
Of mixed messages.
Which is the best
Advice?
           Easy,
Both.
           Let go
And you move
With the world
And its ways.

Hold on
And you're
Honoring the heart.

Do both and you
Live
In the impossible,

Feasting on poems.

*

Oh to be deeply naked
And still see love
In the beloved's eyes.
To be free of shame.

Was there anything
More wonderful?

How long did it last?
Maybe only a moment;
Maybe it was a dream.
We were afraid
To feel such joy.

Still, it changed us,
And for once we knew
We belonged in the world.

*

Easy to agree
Because you always
Knew it was so.
Nodding the head,
Acknowledging
The truth of it:

The beloved
At your life's center—

Whether presence
Or absence,
Star or hollow.

Around it you orbit,
Toward it you bow.

*

It's our bravest deed—
To wed the world.

Espousing the beloved
Takes courage.

Virgil called them
"The tears of things,"
And I think I know
What he means—

Sometimes it seems
All of nature weeps—
And my best hope
Would be to seek
Release by cutting
Each bright thread
That binds me
To the world.
                    But then
The beloved returns—
As person or place
Or poem or song—
And just as suddenly
I know I belong.

*

Not deepest grief,
Of course—
Nothing can help you
With that.
                    Later
Maybe but not now.
Now you are unreachable,
Alone with all that was
Awry between you.

Alone with what was said
And not said.

Saying it all
Now, freely confessing
What you withheld then,
Admitting what you denied
Only a short while ago.

How obvious that you
Were often wrong and unkind.

Aware now of all the good
Deeds you intended
That remained undone.
Aware of all the good
Between you
That death has undone.

*

All of it's tidal:

The wound
Is how
The world gets in.

The word
Is how
It gets back out.

Ebb and flow
And yet—

When the shards
Speak

It's wholeness
They seek.

Nesting dolls. Inside the body
Of the beloved, the body
Of the Book;
                    Inside that:
The body of the world.

Next time you look
It's all reversed.

                    *

Small Ode to the Beloved

We must worship the beloved in all her forms.

Ibn 'Arabi

When I was a child, you
Were my cat.
                    But
Also, you were
More than that—
You were *whatever*
I looked at with wonder.

And early on I sensed
I'd lose you
(And that proved true)
Yet also that somehow
You'd return.

And even then I knew
I'd never be able

To predict
What shape you'd take
Or when you'd come.

All I could do was hope
I'd recognize you
Even if you were disguised,

As you so often are.

*

To become the tree, that's easy.
To be the flower,
Not so hard.
But to become the beloved:
That's not allowed.

The distance between you:
Crucial as the poem
That bridges it.

That space between your two
Bodies, no matter how closely
Pressed:
      It's essential,
It defines what it is to be
In the world:
        Surrounded
By infinite space, balanced
On the point of a pin,
Spinning there, singing your song.

*

It happens periodically—
The beloved
Plunges
Into oceanic gloom.

For that there's no
Sure cure or antidote.

No poem anyone knows
Could keep him afloat.

Nothing left but to take
A deep breath
And join her descent—
The two of you singing the blues.

        *

A few things you might want to know:
I'm not an idiot. I'm not a mystic.
I've read poems since before
Most of the people
On the planet were born.
Have read them and written them, too.
All the time believing they helped
Me live.
      I was right. But
I was also wrong or at least I
Missed a lot.
        Loss seemed to me
The most of it. I believed in love
But I thought its name was loss.
And worse: when I said "life"
I meant "death." When I said "death"
I have no idea what I meant.

But the body is real, and the world
Also. And the body of the beloved
Is a palpable, beautiful thing.

And poems are real: the body
Writes them, thinking of bodies,
Thinking of the world.

                *

I'm not making this stuff up.
Poems teach this.
Taught this
Since the dawn of time:
If life, then death.
If love, then loss.

But the opposite also true.
And even more so
Because of the beloved,
Because of the beloved and you.

                *

Tears and laughter—
Weighing them out,
One against the other.
Sobs and love-sighs:
Trying to separate them,
Putting each on the scales.

What a job!
        The Book's
No help. Clarification,
Catharsis, coherence:

Every poem in the Book
Aspires to these ideals
But to no avail.

It's all there but
Hopelessly jumbled
And muddled—everything
Tossed in the same sack.
You want to sort it out
And come to some conclusion
And instead
You're tossed in, too.

*

Judging a poem—
Is it wheat or chaff?

Only to critics
Does such stuff matter.

Smart or dumb—who
Really cares or knows?

High or low?
It makes no difference.

The head and the heart—
Which one's on top?

Doesn't matter
As long as both take part.

*

When the beloved
Has the blues—
No cheering her up,
No lifting him
From the dumps.

When the beloved
Is the blues,
No keeping her down,
No muffling his voice.
It sounds out
Over the radio waves—
A low moan and a high
Shout.
      She's the guitar-
Sound like the train
Leaving town.
          Moan and yell—
Where is your baby bound?

     *

How is it I'm tired
And the beloved is lively?

Easy answer: the beloved
Is always ready for love.

Can't we rest awhile,
Can't we sleep?
        "You sleep,"
The beloved replies,

"I'll stay up and watch the stars.
I'll become the world."

Has the moon been up there
All these nights
And I never noticed?

A whole week with my nose
To the ground, to the grind.

And the beloved faithfully
Returning each evening
As the moon.

Where have I been?
Who has abandoned whom?

*

Sudden buildup
Of dark clouds;
Wind's roar;
Lightning
Announcing downpour.

Who says the beloved's
Appearance
Can't terrify?
Who says she can't
Arrive as a summer storm?

*

The sun a hot hand
On your body;
The shade, a cool one.

Summer. The beloved
Presses close.

*

Sun-drenched late-
August days
Ripening
The blackberries
Along the driveway.

Avoiding the briars,
Leaning over
The stalks and
Pushing aside
The yellowing leaves . . .

Each morning
The tart juice
Turning a little
Sweeter
As the fruit darkens.

Which is the beloved,
Which is the world.

*

Pinch of time I'm
Given—
Closest
I'll come to the divine.

Thimble of space
I'm
Placed in—
Why not call it grace?

Net I'm trapped by—
Wide
As the sky;
Who am I
To call it a cage?

This life that's all my days.

*

Not to lead us away
From the world
But deeper into it—
To persuade us
She *is* it.

Not all of it, not
Vastness
But some one thing
We love—

Isn't that what he's become?

*

Watching this inchworm
On a dogwood
Twig—how it
Scrunches up
In a cosmic shrug

Then lifts in front
And flings
Its whole length
Forward
In a single green spasm.

Traveling toward
The beloved?

Who cares how
Or when we get there?

              *

Autumn, and the woods
Are a hundred hues.
The world's put on
A parti-colored dress;
The beloved is ready
To rumba.
              The last
Dance or the first?

Hard to say.
The beloved dies
And is reborn
So many times.
                    Dies
And is reborn so many
Ways.
        Tomorrow
Who knows, but
Today she's
These woods
I'm strolling through.

              *

Skitterbugs on the stream's surface.
Poems in the Book.

Zipping here, then there;
Nervous, elusive, shooting off
At absurd angles.
                    Harmless
Creatures. Can't be caught
In the quickest hand.

Silly-looking.
But the water they move on
Is clear and deep.

                    *

Even as we speak
Another one
Vanishes completely,
Goes the way
Of the Carolina parakeet,
The passenger pigeon—
Beloveds whom
It's too late to embrace.

Now not sadness
Or saying
Or rage
Can alter their fate.

We humans must have
Voted
Somewhere
In our secret hearts
That we didn't
Need them.
                    And now
It's true—we don't.

Although our trip
Will be that much
Lonelier
Without them:
                    A whole
Species no more
Than a small
Bright torch
Someone held aloft
As we all
Marched
Into the deepening dark.

And now it's gone out.

                    *

Not a killing frost, only
A cold snap
That briefly revives
Dahlias and asters
And other autumn flowers.

As if they knew:
Not much longer before . . .

As if they sensed
Now
Was the time
To bloom extravagantly.

"Next week?" the beloved
Whispers,
                    "There is no next week."

Humble dazzle
Of autumn:
These leaves
On the ground—
Each one a page
In the Book,
A poem that says:
I lived.
          I was
A small part
Of the whole
Story—this
Is my song,
This is my glory.

Doesn't the world demand
We dance?
Doesn't it insist on it?
And why not?
                    Look
At the leaves,
Look at the weeds.
Look at the least blade
Of grass in the breeze.

None of them begs off
Or offers excuses.

None of them refuses.

To praise what's there:
Isn't that prayer?

The world spread out
Before us—

What else should we adore?

*

Autumn and the days
Grow shorter;
Squeezing the same radiance
Into a smaller space.

More intense than ever,
The beloved's lust for us.

She must know
We, too, are getting ready
To become a poem.

*

Let me be the first
To admit it—
Our relationship
Was often difficult

Filled with
Unfortunate
Misunderstandings
And infinite
Failures on my part

Take for instance
Photosynthesis—
A concept
I never fully
Grasped
Though I knew
It was
Essential to you

Still you must
Believe me
O verdant
Earth
O green world

It was you
It was always you

*

How radiant and pale
The winter sycamore branches
From which the outer bark
Has peeled and fallen
Like gray rags.
                    What a gift
That the leaves do not
Obscure its nakedness.

The risen body. The risen
Body of the beloved
Still in this world.

*

How the crocus pops up:
Leafless stalk and purple
Blossom-cup out of bare mud!

As if it couldn't wait any longer.
Not even the grass has ventured forth.
Ice and snow could still return.

What does the beloved care?
So eager to begin again,
To welcome the new life.

*

The dandelion, too.
First, it's a plush sun,
Then, before you know it,
It's become a ghostly globe—
And of its two forms
Who can say
Which is more lovely?

As if you had to choose
Between the glorious world
And the words that resurrect it.

*

Here I am, sitting on the porch
Of my cottage,
Wearing a pair
Of bright new socks
That you might think
You recognize
From Pablo Neruda's ode,

But these are a pair
I bought myself
So my feet could be
Warm on a cool
May morning like this.

The socks aren't cool at all,
But "hot," with swirling
Bands of red and blue
Like a psychedelic
Barber pole except
There is no white
And so no irony about
The American flag,
Although
They were probably
Knitted by some
Poor son of a bitch
On a huge machine in China—
A former peasant
Who now works
A fifteen-hour shift
And sleeps in a small room
In the factory dormitory
With ten others who don't
Even speak his dialect—
And all for pennies a day
And a thousand miles
From his mountain home,
While I sit here in Virginia
And pull on these bright socks
Against the late May chill.

Nor is my ode about
Imperialist guilt
Or even its dark twin—
The global economy—
Because after all, they
Will win soon, and someday
His descendants
Will feel they rule
This foolish and suffering world.

So I'm guessing the moral
Of my ode has more to do
With the mystery
Of it all:
          How being alive
Is probably the best
That most of us
Can accomplish,
Though gratitude
For what we've received
Is the least we can feel,
Not to mention compassion
For those
Who suffer endlessly,

Who may never get a glimpse
Or wink of joy.
               And my luck
Seems double luck
Because it's so gratuitous,
Because I never did a thing
To earn it and yet
It's come to me, as has
This morning

With its early light slanting
Through maple trees
Alive with birdcalls
And me looking out
On the innocent day
With the eyes I was given for free.

FROM The Second Book of the Book,
Which Is the Body of the Beloved
Which Is the World

Long night on the road.
Huge distance between
Two cities.
                    Distance also
Between radio stations.
Only static coming through.

Stop for coffee at this diner.
Need to wake up. Need
To consult the little book
Of the jukebox and hear
The beloved sing my song.

                    *

Snow on the mountain
This January morning
Though the sky's blue.
Must have fallen
Last night.

More gray hairs
On my head
Every month.
My mustache
Almost completely
White now.

Too many funerals,
Not enough weddings.
Not enough birth
Announcements.

I hope the beloved
Isn't losing ground.

*

Naked before the beloved.

And the beloved naked
Before us.
                    No wonder
The censors get excited.

No wonder the Book
Is seldom mentioned,

Not readily available,
Difficult and risky to find.

No wonder we search for it
All our days.
                    No wonder
We seek just a glimpse of it,

And catching that glimpse,
Are changed.

*

Parched and wizened—
We who feared
Love
Would never come—
And now this flood.

What shall we do
With the surplus,
With the overflow?

Give it away,
Give it away.

How much more
Than we can absorb
The beloved bestows.

                *

Such a shaking. If the elbows
Were held by nuts and bolts
We'd have rattled apart.

But sinew and socket kept
Their grip; the body's intact.

And to think: a poem did that.

                *

The poem didn't express
Emotion, it *was* emotion.
And so was I
As I became the poem
As I read it aloud
As I rose from my daily grave.

                *

No one I ever believed said:
"There is no death."

Besides, I don't want to live
Forever.
            Already I'm forgetting
Things: not just names and dates

But also moments and places
I cherished.
                    And I'm feeling
Old: certain parts
Of my body always ache.

"To love forever." Now that's
A different matter. That's
What the Book teaches me;
That's why I keep reading.

                    *

Tired of the body?
Tired of the poem
Of the body?
                    Rest awhile.
Even the most passionate
Lovers paused.
                    Even
The fiercest warriors
Put down their swords,
Exhausted by slaughter.

                    *

There are sorrows
So large
You can stand
Inside them.

There are losses
That open
Wounds
Far too
Wide to stitch.

That said, don't
Forget:
          The road
Made of poems
Connecting
Hope and hurt—

It's a two-way route.

                    *

Who else can do it—
Discover that secret
Constellation
That rules our days?

Certain poems scattered
Here and there
In the Book—
Those we most love:

Urgent stars
It's up to us to connect.

                    *

Calm down, calm down.
But why calm down?
When I'm dead and only
A poem in the Book
Read by someone
Not yet born:
Then I'll be calm.
Then I'll tell them
In a quiet voice

What a miracle it is
To be alive. I won't
Shout and jump around.
I'll whisper it in her ear.

And if I'm lucky
She'll shout and jump
Around; her heart
Will beat a little faster.

*

He's the answer
That arrives
Before
We pose the question.

She's the fish
That swims up
Before the net is woven.

Wake up, wake up!

To be ready
For the beloved,
You need both eyes open.

*

Today only a single poem.
This one.
So small.

In the Middle Ages
Angels frolicked
On the head of a pin—
Spacious as a ballroom.

Have faith.
The beloved approaches,
Robed in radiance,
Dressed in language,
Eager to dance.

*

The Book said we were mortal;
It didn't say we had to be morbid.

The Book said the beloved died,
But also that she comes again,
That he's reborn as words.

The Book said: everything perishes.
The Book said: that's why we sing.

*

You can read the world
Without words:
Eyes take in its dazzle.

And you can read the body
Of the beloved by touch.

You can do that much
And all of it magic, but
Neither body nor world
Can be born again
Except by tongue.

And to live once only—
What if that's not enough?

When Sappho wrote:
"Whatever one loves most
Is beautiful," she began
The poems of heart's praise
Which make up the Book
Of the body of the beloved
Which is the world.

Everything in the Book
Flows from that single poem

Or the countless others
That say the same thing
In other words, other ways.

*

Cool to the touch
Yet containing such
Heat at its heart.

Full of words but
Most so simple—
Is anything
Going on in its head?

The Book's a mystery
That all your
Thinking won't solve.

Best to read and feel.

*

Memorize those lines you love
As you tried to memorize
Every part of the beloved's body.

Memorize, and then forget—
Let them vanish
Into that dark that's large as death.

They'll come again
When you most need, least expect.

                    *

You might think the things I say
Are too simple for words,
Too embarrassing to be spoken.

But if I repeat the obvious,
Where's the harm in that?

Maybe it was always simple:
Loss surrounds us.
Who would deny it?

We ourselves are loss, are lost.
But those who came before us
Left the Book as a guide,
The book full of songs and poems.

                    *

When you're afraid,
You're afraid
Of something.

When you dread,
It's Nothing
That you dread
(So the philosopher
Said).
          Nothing
Can be
Terrifying—
But don't get
Confused: a blank
Page in the Book
Isn't Nothing.

It's something
Waiting to happen;
It's the beloved
Holding her breath,
Hoping you'll write or call.

                    *

A thousand years ago
A poet glimpsed
The beloved
And felt his eyes
Fill with tears,
Felt his mouth
Become a smile.

From what depths
Inside you
Do they rise
As you read
That poem aloud—
Those tears

In your eyes now,
That same smile.

*

Too many mysteries. Too many
Emotions. Why don't we stop
Adding to the Book?
Why don't we let it rest
In neglect for a few generations?

Could we? Is it in our power?

I've sat by it and seen it expand
Without anyone opening
Its covers.

I've seen it grow as if someone
Had merely thought a poem.

*

Wildness of the world,
Branches tossing in a storm.
Yet the beloved seemed so mild,
Seemed calm at the center
Even when passion swept her,
Even when he lost control.

Quiet surface of the world
And wildness at the center:
The beloved gazes in a mirror
That turns everything inside out.

And the Book. Sometimes
It's a rock. Sometimes
Its wings frantically beat
Inside an invisible cage.

*

It's not as if I didn't
Know the rules.
I as good as
Signed
A contract:

"Here only once.

No moment
To be
Repeated."

Bowing the head,
Accepting
That fact

Then lifting the head
Again,

Opening
The eyes
So as to see
Both this and that.

*

Did the beloved die?
Yes and no.
Only really ceasing
When we cease to care.

Therefore (as Keats put it)
"On every morrow,
Are we wreathing
A flowery band
To bind us to the earth."

Which is to say:
Composing poems
And melodious songs
That celebrate the world.

Which is to say:
Helping the beloved
To be reborn
By writing and reading
Poems.

Which is to say:
We have an urgent purpose.

Which is to say.

                    *

You lost the beloved.
You thought:
                    Her page
Is torn from the book
Of life.

You thought:
It's as if he never lived.

How wrong you were!
Loss writes so many
Poems in the Book,
Writes till its hand aches,
Till it's exhausted
And can't write anymore.

Then it sings a song.

*

When you're sad
The Book grows larger
As if to comfort you.

When you despair
It can narrow
To a single poem.

And when joy
Arrives—hard
To read at all.
Blinking at
Page-dazzle;
The words
Breaking apart
Into letters,
Dancing there,
Unable to calm down.

*

What or whom does the Book
Exclude?
         Nothing and no one.

Not a single leaf on a tree.
Not an eyelash.
Not a tear or a smile.

It welcomes all the beloveds.
Shelters them,
Shapes them into words.

Then gives them back,
Gives them back to the world.

*

If we could have the world
Without the beloved,
Would that suffice?

Lacks one, lacks both.
Did you think that heap
Of objects was the world?

It only becomes the world
Because of the beloved:

She lends it her light;
His kiss makes it live.

*

Making light of the beloved—
Laughing not *at* her
But *with* her,
Laughing at death
Even.
       Making light
Of the beloved—
Turning the mortal dark
Into radiant words.

Making light of the beloved
Because he weighs
Almost nothing.

Lifting him easily,
As you lift a book;
Balancing her
On the tip of your tongue.

         *

How to exhaust the inexhaustible?
The world can't stop giving.
Nor can the beloved.

When the beloved dies
It's only to ask more of you
So you become richer from giving.

         *

Refute the resurrection
Of the beloved?
Why not argue
With a bush

In spring
As it begins
Pushing out
Its green leaves?
Why not
Cross-examine
The robin's song?

Logic—that's not
Passion's language.
The brain alone
Is an old turtle.
It needs its pond
And its log. It needs
The body and the heart.

*

High Virginia summer,
And where
Is the beloved?

Almost buried
By this thick green.

How can she breathe
Under such luxuriance?

Perfume of honeysuckle
And the pink taffy
Flowers of mimosa.

Humid morning—
Close as a room
With a corpse.

But the beloved's there,
Keeping still
Because of the heat.

His heart beating slow
But still beating.

*

The river has a single song,
Which is itself.
The tree has a song.
The bird also.
The heart knows all
These songs
And a million of its own.

Neither the river
Nor the bird can write.
The tree moves
Its branches against
The sky all day
As if it were thinking
About inventing
Its own alphabet—
But nothing comes of it.

So it's still up to us.
We're supposed to bring
Them into the Book,
Make a place for them in our poems.

*

So many singers
And only the one song.

So many songs
And just the one singer.

So many beloveds,
So many songs—

And this: our only world.

*

Now the leaves are falling fiercely,
Giving themselves to the wind's
Will like a Technicolor blizzard.

Safe in my house looking out.
Savoring the poem of wildness,
Savoring the world's unthinking
Decision to give itself over entirely.

This window between me and the world:
Like reading a page in the Book,
Taking it in deeply.
                    Gladdened
By the swirl and swoop of it,
Gladdened by this emblem of passion.

Glad also of the glass, of the distance
That makes it safe to feel this.

*

Lingering over it,
Wanting to make it last
Longer.
   Still,
It ends.

No joy
That doesn't cease.
No life that goes on
Forever.

The poet writes
Then puts down
His pen.

The singer comes
To the end
Of her song.

Autumn now:
The leaves falling.

Beautiful world
That persists
When words stop.

Beautiful words
That lift the world
In a song of praise
That drifts
Like a leaf in a breeze.

   *

Nazim Hikmet begins a poem
With the phrase: "Another thing
I didn't know I loved."
He writes in a tone of amazement.

He's a Turkish poet in exile.
He's on a train in winter,
Leaving Prague and headed
Toward an uncertain future.
The poem he's writing is a list
Of things he suddenly knows
Are precious.
                    He's not sure
Where he's going—old man
At the start of a long, cold ride.
The list he recites is also long.

As long as he keeps making that list,
He's traveling toward the beloved.

*

When the beloved appears
As a daylily
She has only one
Arc of the sun
To blossom, to blare
The orange trumpet
Of her being
Loudly into the world.

Quick, write a poem—
We must prolong her song.

*

No postmortems, please.
The world is immortal.
The world renews itself.

What about poems and songs—
Do they perish?
Maybe they only
Vanish awhile;
Maybe they go underground
To gather some other
Knowledge and come back
In another form:

New words, a new melody,
Yet somehow
The same beloved
Singing the same song.

*

Sorrow and joy—
Stars
We steer by.

Love and loss,
Guiding
Us on.

Lured on
Journeys—
Outward we roam.

The farther
We travel,
The closer to home.

*

Listening to Bach's suites
For cello, you know
He's found the poem
But not the words,
Doesn't need the words.

And the words don't matter
When the mother weeps
Over her dead child.

Some of the most important
Poems don't get written down,
But you'll find them in the Book.

*

That single line: a rope
The poem tossed out
Into the dark,
Into the river's swirl.

You're holding one end;
The beloved, the other.

Rescue is imminent.

Too soon to say whose.

*

Song on the jukebox—
An emissary
The beloved sent—
It's only doing
Its two-part job:

First, it breaks our heart;

Then it promises
Never to mend it again.

               *

Thirsty?
        The poem
Is a cup of water.

Hungry?
        The song
Is a loaf of bread.

"Only in imagination,"
The skeptic said.

True, true.
        But it—
It above all—must be fed.

               *

I confess it—I've been
Lazy for days,
Wandering around
Lost in the maze
Of spring's profusions;
Writing

These poems
And neglecting my garden.

I heard the willow
Singing
And imagined
It was the beloved.

I listened to the frogs'
Chorus
And thought so again.

Neglecting so much
And now
My comeuppance:

A wren built its nest
In my weeding basket
That hangs
By a hook
In the open shed—

Three round, pale eggs!

*

Do words outlast
The world
They describe?
Do the things
Fall away,
Leaving only
The husks
Of their names?

And what does
Their perishing
Ask of us?

Lift up, lift up:
A song
Could redeem them,
A poem
Could fill them
With life again.

Don't we owe
The world
At least that much
That gave itself
So freely to us?

*

Who wants to talk
When they can listen?

Who wants to listen
Rather than talk?

The Book talks all
The time, but
It's also listening.

What could we tell
The Book
That it hasn't
Already heard?

Yet it savors all
We say,
Savors every word.

*

Body of the beloved,
Body of the world.

The eyes can't cease
Their feasting.

Book of the body
Of the beloved:
Inexhaustible.

Not just the Book
But also your hunger for it.

*

Spasm and sadness.
A little kiss, then
A little chasm.

It could give passion
A bad name.

Luckily, the Book
Has a thing or two
To say about this.

*

Acrobatic postures I enjoyed
In my youth but
Can't even imagine now.

I could study this crude
Drawing for hours and still
Not figure out how it's done.

Some secrets and joys
Time takes downriver,
Never to be seen again.

Behind me forever:
Both the temptations of youth
And its strenuous attempts.

Settling now for the Book's
Calmer sections and pleasures.

*

In the spring swamp,
The red-winged blackbird
Perched on a cattail stalk—
Have you heard its song?
If you have, no need of heaven,
No need of divine resurrection.

It's one of those birdsongs
That holds a spot in the Book,
Saving that space until
A human song comes along
Worthy to replace
All that wordless love.

Lucky poets us
To whom
Sappho bequeathed
Her voodoo lute

That we might name
And praise
And raise from oblivion's
Grave

All that we most love.

*

Being being nothing
But breath

And the fog it makes
On the windowpane,

Which is a page
In the Book

On which
You write your name.

*

Squander it all!
Hold nothing back.

The heart's a deep well.

And when it's empty
It will fill again.

A song of resurrection played
On a leg-bone flute?
I don't think so.

We want more than to just
Make the dust dance;
We want the beloved's
Living presence
Returned to us as song.

Hair, lips, brows, the beautiful
Flesh and features: words
Can evoke them; poems
Can bring them again
To the mind's eye.

Hollow bone into which
We breathe our sorrow.
No, that won't do.
                    Something
So empty, but it's not emptiness
We feel.
          I think we must
Ourselves become
Both instrument and song,
Full as we are with longing.

*

This is what was bequeathed us:
This earth the beloved left
And, leaving,
Left to us.

No other world
But this one:
Willows and the river
And the factory
With its black smokestacks.

No other shore, only this bank
On which the living gather.

No meaning but what we find here.
No purpose but what we make.

That, and the beloved's clear instructions:
Turn me into song, sing me awake.

Index of Titles

Index of First Lines

About the Author

Gregory Orr is the author of twelve collections of poetry, most recently *The Last Love Poem I Will Ever Write* (Norton 2019). Milkweed Editions recently reissued his memoir, *The Blessing* (2019). His prose books include *A Primer for Poets and Readers of Poetry* (Norton, 2018) and *Poetry as Survival* (University of Georgia Press, 2002). At the Dodge Poetry Festival in 2018, he premiered a fifty-minute song/poem cycle, "The Beloved," with the Parkington Sisters. He's been interviewed by Krista Tippett for her "On Being" series, by PBS NewsHour, and by NPR's "This I Believe" series. Orr has published op-ed pieces in the *New York Times* on gun violence, trauma, and his experiences as a volunteer in the civil rights movement in the sixties. He has received fellowships from the Guggenheim Foundation and the National Endowment for the Arts and an Award in Literature from the American Academy of Arts and Letters. Professor Emeritus at the University of Virginia, Orr taught there from 1975–2019 and was founder and first director of its MFA Program in Writing. He lives with his wife, the painter Trisha Orr, in Charlottesville, Virginia.

Poetry is vital to language and living. Since 1972, Copper Canyon Press has published extraordinary poetry from around the world to engage the imaginations and intellects of readers, writers, booksellers, librarians, teachers, students, and donors.

COPPER CANYON PRESS WISHES TO EXTEND A SPECIAL THANKS
TO THE FOLLOWING SUPPORTERS WHO PROVIDED FUNDING
DURING THE COVID-19 PANDEMIC:

Academy of American Poets (Literary Relief Fund)
City of Seattle Office of Arts & Culture
Community of Literary Magazines and Presses (Literary Relief Fund)
Economic Development Council of Jefferson County
4Culture
National Book Foundation (Literary Relief Fund)
Poetry Foundation
U.S. Department of the Treasury Payroll Protection Program

WE ARE GRATEFUL FOR THE MAJOR SUPPORT
PROVIDED BY:

academy of american poets

THE PAUL G. ALLEN FAMILY FOUNDATION

amazon literary partnership

the point envision·enact·evolve

Lannan

4 CULTURE

A&

OFFICE OF ARTS & CULTURE
SEATTLE

National Endowment for the Arts arts.gov
ART WORKS.

WASHINGTON STATE ARTS COMMISSION

The Witter Bynner Foundation for Poetry

TO LEARN MORE ABOUT UNDERWRITING
COPPER CANYON PRESS TITLES,
PLEASE CALL 360-385-4925 EXT. 103

WE ARE GRATEFUL FOR THE MAJOR SUPPORT
PROVIDED BY:

Richard Andrews
Anonymous (3)
Jill Baker and Jeffrey Bishop
Anne and Geoffrey Barker
In honor of Ida Bauer, Betsy
    Gifford, and Beverly Sachar
Donna Bellew
Matthew Bellew
Sarah Bird
Will Blythe
John Branch
Diana Broze
John R. Cahill
Sarah Cavanaugh
Stephanie Ellis-Smith and
    Douglas Smith
Austin Evans
Saramel Evans
Mimi Gardner Gates
Gull Industries Inc. on behalf of
    William True
The Trust of Warren A. Gummow
William R. Hearst III
Carolyn and Robert Hedin
David and Jane Hibbard
Bruce Kahn
Phil Kovacevich and Eric Wechsler

Lakeside Industries Inc. on behalf
    of Jeanne Marie Lee
Maureen Lee and Mark Busto
Peter Lewis and Johnna Turiano
Ellie Mathews and Carl Youngmann
    as The North Press
Larry Mawby and Lois Bahle
Hank and Liesel Meijer
Jack Nicholson
Gregg Orr
Petunia Charitable Fund and
    adviser Elizabeth Hebert
Suzanne Rapp and Mark Hamilton
Adam and Lynn Rauch
Emily and Dan Raymond
Joseph C. Roberts
Jill and Bill Ruckelshaus
Cynthia Sears
Kim and Jeff Seely
Joan F. Woods
Barbara and Charles Wright
In honor of C.D. Wright,
    from Forrest Gander
Caleb Young as C. Young Creative
The dedicated interns and
    faithful volunteers of
    Copper Canyon Press

The Chinese character for poetry is made up of two parts:
"word" and "temple." It also serves as pressmark for
Copper Canyon Press.

The poems are set in Adobe Garamond Pro.
Book design and composition by Phil Kovacevich.